CHRISTMAS THOUGHTS

J. C. Ryle

Edited by

Andrew Atherstone

THE BANNER OF TRUTH TRUST

THE BANNER OF TRUTH TRUST

Head Office
3 Murrayfield Road
Edinburgh, EH12 6EL
UK

North America Office
610 Alexander Spring Road
Carlisle, PA 17015
USA

banneroftruth.org

© The Banner of Truth Trust 2022
First published in 2022
Reprinted 2023

★

ISBN
Print: 978 1 80040 314 7
Epub: 978 1 80040 315 4
Kindle: 978 1 80040 316 1

★

Typeset in 12/15 Bembo at
The Banner of Truth Trust, Edinburgh

Printed in the USA
by Versa Press Inc.
East Peoria, IL

Contents

Introduction

John Ryle was a warm-hearted pastor and preacher in rural Suffolk, vicar of the little villages of Helmingham and Stradbroke. Often at Christmas and New Year he wrote an exhortation to his parishioners in the form of a short tract, distributed from house to house. These tracts were hugely popular, eagerly read in towns and villages across England, each running into multiple editions in tens of thousands of copies.

Christmas, and New Year, are excellent moments to pause and reflect—as scattered families regather for the national holiday, and as the calendar turns over again, with another year gone forever. Ryle urges us—in the midst of our feasting and festivities and family reunions—to make time to consider our spiritual state and our relationship with God. How is it with our souls? What do we make of Jesus Christ? What will be our future, when all our Christmases are past?

This little book contains five of Ryle's most popular Christmas tracts, originally published during the 1850s and 1860s. They have not been issued in this Christmas form since they were first printed more than a century and a half ago. Ryle writes in classic Victorian style, but with a freshness and crispness and direct appeal to readers in every generation. The spiritual wisdom of these Christmas Thoughts is timeless. Ryle challenges us—while we enjoy the wonderful delights of mince pies and mistletoe and mulled wine and music and merriment—to make the most of every Christmas, to consider seriously the person of Jesus Christ and questions of eternal significance.

ANDREW ATHERSTONE
Oxford

Come!
A Christmas Invitation

———

'*Come unto me, all ye that labour and are heavy laden, and I will give you rest.*'—Matthew 11:28

Reader,

The name of the tract before you is short. But the subject which the name unfolds is deeply important. It is the first word of a text of Scripture which deserves to be written in letters of gold. I offer that text to you as a Christmas invitation. I entreat you to look at it, and ponder it well. That single text may be the salvation of your soul.

The end of another year is close at hand. Another Christmas is drawing near. Family parties are once more gathering. Friends are inviting friends to come and see them. Homes are being filled with happy faces. Surely, at a time like this, *an invitation* cannot be out of season! Listen, then, to the invitation which I bring you this day. It may be unlike any that you have yet received. But it is of unspeakable importance. It concerns the eternal happiness of your soul.

Reader, do not shrink back when you read these words. I do not want to spoil your Christmas pleasures, provided always that your pleasures are not mixed with sin. I know that there is a time to laugh, as well as a time to weep. But I do want you to be thoughtful, as well as happy—to consider, as well as to make mirth. There are some missing at Christmas parties this winter, who a year ago were alive and well. There are some now gathering round Christmas firesides, who a year hence will be lying in their graves.

Reader, how long have you yourself to live? Will another Christmas find you alive? Once more I entreat you to listen to the invitation which I bring you this day. I have a message for you from my Master. He says, 'Come unto me all ye that labour and are heavy-laden, and I will give you rest.'

There are four points in the text before you, to which I ask your attention. On each of these I have somewhat to say.

I. First. *Who is the Speaker of this invitation?*
II. Secondly. *To whom is this invitation addressed?*
III. Thirdly. *What does the Speaker ask us to do?*
IV. Lastly. *What does the Speaker offer to give?*

May the Holy Ghost bless the reading of this tract to your everlasting benefit! May this Christmas prove the happiest and best Christmas you have ever spent!

I. In the first place, *Who is the Speaker of the invitation which heads this tract?* Who is it that invites so freely, and offers so largely? Who is it that says to your conscience this day, 'Come—come unto me'?

Reader, you have a right to ask these questions. You live in a dying world. The earth is full of cheats, shams, deceptions, impositions and falsehoods. The value of a promissory note depends entirely on the name which is signed at the bottom. When you hear of a mighty Promiser you have a right to say, Who is this? and what is his name?

The speaker of the invitation before you is the greatest and best friend that man has ever had. It is the Lord Jesus Christ, the eternal Son of God.

He is one who is *almighty*. He is God the Father's fellow and equal. He is very God of very God. By him were all things made. In his hand are all the treasures of wisdom and knowledge. He has all power in heaven and earth. In him all fulness dwells. He has the keys of death and hell. He is now the appointed mediator between God and man. He will one day be the judge and king of all the earth. Reader, when such an one as this speaks, you may safely trust him. What he promises he is able to perform.

He is one who is *most loving*. He loved us so that he left heaven for our sakes, and laid aside for a season the glory that he had with the Father. He loved us so that he was born of a woman for our sakes, and lived thirty-three years in this sinful world. He loved us so that he undertook to pay our mighty debt to God, and died upon the cross to make atonement for our sins. Reader, when such an one as this speaks, he deserves a hearing. When he promises a thing, you need not be afraid to trust him.

He is one who *knows the heart of man* most thoroughly. He took on him a body like our own, and was made like man in all things, sin only excepted. He knows by experience what man has to go through. He has tasted poverty, and weariness, and hunger, and thirst, and pain, and temptation. He is acquainted with all our condition upon earth. He has 'suffered himself being tempted.'[1] Reader,

[1] Hebrews 2:18.

when such an one as this makes an offer, he makes it with perfect wisdom. He knows exactly what you and I need.

He is one who *never breaks his word*. He always fulfils his promises. He never fails to do what he undertakes. He never disappoints the soul that trusts him. Mighty as he is, there is one thing which he cannot do. It is impossible for him to lie. Reader, when such an one as this makes a promise, you need not doubt that he will stand to it. You may depend with confidence on his word.

Reader, you have now heard who sends you the invitation which is before you today. It is the Lord Jesus Christ. Give him the credit due to his name. Grant him a full and impartial hearing. Believe that a promise from his mouth deserves your best attention. See that you refuse not him that speaketh. It is written, 'If they escaped not who refused him that spake on earth, much more shall not we escape if we refuse him that speaketh from heaven' (Hebrews 12:25).

II. I will now show you, in the second place, *to whom the invitation before you is addressed*.

The Lord Jesus Christ addresses 'all that labour and are heavy laden.' The expression is deeply comforting and instructive. It is wide, sweeping, and comprehensive. It describes the case of millions in every part of the world.

Where are the labouring and heavy laden? They are everywhere. They are a multitude that man can scarcely number. They are to be found in every climate, and in every country under the sun. They live in Europe, in Asia, in Africa, and in America. They dwell by the banks of the Seine, as well as the banks of the Thames—by the banks of the Mississippi as well as the banks of the Niger. They abound under republics as well as under monarchies—under liberal governments as well as under despotism. Everywhere you will find trouble, care, sorrow, anxiety, murmuring, discontent, and unrest. What does it mean? What does it all come to? Men are 'labouring and heavy laden.'

To what class do the labouring and heavy laden belong? They belong to every class: there is no exception. They are to be found among masters as well as among servants—among rich as well as among poor—among kings as well as among subjects—among learned as among ignorant. In every class you will find trouble, care, sorrow, anxiety, murmuring, discontent, and unrest. What does it mean? What does it all come to? Men are 'labouring and heavy laden.'

Reader, how shall we explain this? What is the cause of the state of things which I have just tried to describe? Did God create man at the beginning to be unhappy? Most certainly not. Are human governments to blame because men are not happy? At most to a very slight extent. The fault lies far too deep to be reached by human laws. There is another cause, a cause which many unhappily refuse to see. That cause is sin.

Reader, sin and departure from God are the true reasons why men are everywhere labouring and heavy laden. Sin is the universal disease which infects the whole earth. Sin brought in thorns and thistles at the beginning, and obliged man to earn his bread by the sweat of his brow. Sin is the reason why the whole creation groaneth and travaileth in pain, and the foundations of the earth are out of course.[2] Sin is the cause of all the burdens which now press down mankind. Most men know it not, and weary themselves in vain to explain the state of things around them. But sin is the great root and foundation of all sorrow, whatever proud man may think. How much men ought to hate sin!

Reader, are you one of those who are labouring and heavy laden? I think it very likely that you are.

---

[2] Romans 8:22; Psalm 82:5.

I am firmly persuaded that there are thousands of men and women in the world who are inwardly uncomfortable, and yet will not confess it. They feel a burden on their hearts, which they would gladly get rid of; and yet they do not know the way. They have a conviction that all is not right in their inward man, which they never tell to anyone. Husbands do not tell it to their wives, and wives do not tell it to their husbands. Children do not tell it to their parents, and friends do not tell it to their friends. But the inward burden lies heavily on many hearts! There is far more unhappiness than the world sees. Disguise it as some will, there are multitudes uncomfortable because they know they are not prepared to meet God. And you, who are reading this tract, perhaps are one.

Reader, if you are labouring, and heavy laden, you are the very person to whom the Lord Jesus Christ sends an invitation this day. If you have an aching heart, and a sore conscience—if you want rest for a weary soul, and know not where to find it—if you want peace for a guilty heart, and are at a loss which way to turn—you are the man, you are the woman, to whom Jesus speaks today. There is hope for you. I bring you good tidings. 'Come unto me,' says the Lord Jesus, 'and I will give you rest.'

You may tell me this invitation cannot be meant for you, because you are not good enough to be invited by Christ. I answer, that Jesus does not speak to the good, but to the labouring and heavy laden. Do you know anything of this feeling? Then you are one to whom he speaks.

You may tell me that the invitation cannot be meant for you, because you are a sinner, and know nothing about religion. I answer, that it matters nothing what you are, or what you have been. Do you at this moment feel labouring and heavy laden? Then you are one to whom Jesus speaks.

You may tell me that you cannot think the invitation is meant for you, because you are not yet converted, and have not got a new heart. I answer that Christ's invitation is not addressed to the converted, but to the labouring and heavy laden. Is this what you feel? Is there any burden on your heart? Then you are one of those to whom Christ speaks.

You may tell me that you have no right to accept this invitation, because you do not know that you are one of God's elect. I answer, that you have no right to put words in Christ's mouth, which he has not used. He does not say, 'Come unto me, all ye that are elect.' He addresses all the labouring and heavy-laden ones without any exception. Are you one of them? Is there weight within on your soul? This is the only question you have to decide. If you are, you are one of those to whom Christ speaks.

Reader, if you are one of the labouring and heavy-laden ones, once more I entreat you not to refuse the invitation which I bring you today. Do not forsake your own mercies. The harbour of refuge is freely before you. Do not turn away from it. The best of friends holds out his hand to you. Let not pride, or self-righteousness, or fear of man's ridicule, make you reject his proffered love. Take him at his word. Say to him, 'Lord Jesus Christ, I am one of those whom thine invitation suits. I am labouring and heavy laden. Lord, what wilt thou have me to do?'

III. I will now show you, in the third place, *what the Lord Jesus Christ asks you to do*. Three words make up the sum and substance of the invitation which he sends you today. If you are labouring and heavy laden, Jesus says, 'Come unto me.'

Reader, there is a grand simplicity about the three words now before you. Short and plain as the sentence seems, it contains a mine of deep truth and solid comfort. Weigh it. Look at it. Consider it. Ponder it well. I believe that it is one half of saving Christianity to understand what Jesus means, when he says, 'Come unto me.'

Mark well, that the Lord Jesus does not bid the labouring and heavy laden 'go and work.' Those words would carry no comfort to heavy consciences. It would be like requiring labour from an exhausted man. No! He bids them 'Come.' He does not say, 'Pay me what thou owest.' That demand would drive a broken heart into despair. It would be like claiming a debt from a ruined bankrupt. No! He says, 'Come.' He does not say, 'Stand still and wait.' That command would only be a mockery. It would be like promising to give medicine at the end of a week to one at the point of death. No! He says, 'Come!' Today—at once—without any delay, 'Come unto me.'

But, after all, what is meant by coming to Christ? It is an expression often used, but often misunderstood. Beware that you make no mistake at this point. Here unhappily, thousands turn aside out of the right course, and miss the truth. Beware that you do not make shipwreck at the very mouth of the harbour.

Take notice, that coming to Christ means something more than coming to church and chapel. You may fill your place regularly at a place of worship, and attend all outward means of grace, and yet not be saved. All this is not coming to Christ.

Take notice, that coming to Christ is something more than coming to the Lord's table. You may be a regular member and communicant. You may never be missing in the lists of those who eat that bread and drink that wine, which the Lord commanded to be received, and yet you may never be saved. All this is not coming to Christ.

Take notice, that coming to Christ is something more than coming to ministers. You may be a constant hearer of some popular preacher, and a zealous partisan of all his opinions, and yet never be saved. All this is not coming to Christ.

Take notice, once more, that coming to Christ is something more than coming to the possession of head-knowledge about him. You may know the whole system of evangelical doctrine, and be able to talk, argue, and dispute on every jot of it, and yet never be saved. All this is not coming to Christ.

Coming to Christ is coming to him with the heart by simple faith. Believing on Christ is coming to him, and coming to Christ is believing on him. It is that act of the soul which takes place when a man, feeling his own sins, and despairing of all other hope, commits himself to Christ for salvation, ventures on him, trusts him, and casts himself wholly on him. When a man turns to Christ empty that he may be filled—sick that he may be healed—hungry that he may be satisfied—thirsty that he may be refreshed—needy that he may be enriched—dying that he may have life—lost that he may be saved—guilty that he may be pardoned—sin-defiled that he may be cleansed—confessing that Christ alone can supply his need—then he comes to Christ. When he uses Christ as the Jews used the city of refuge—as the starving Egyptians used Joseph—as the dying Israelites used the brazen serpent—then he comes to Christ. It is the empty soul's venture on a full Saviour. It is the drowning man's grasp on the hand held out to help him. It is the sick man's reception of a healing medicine. This, and nothing more than this, is coming to Christ.

Hearken, my beloved reader, whoever you may be, hearken to a word of caution. Beware of mistakes as to this matter of coming to Christ. Do not stop short in any half-way house. Do not allow the devil and the world to cheat you out of eternal life. Do not suppose that you will ever get any good from Christ, unless you go straight, direct, thoroughly, and entirely to Christ himself. Trust not in a little outward formality. Content not yourself with a regular use of outward means.

A lantern is an excellent help in a dark night, but it is not home. Means of grace are useful aids, but they are not Christ. Oh, no! Press onward, forward, upward, till you have had personal, business-like dealings with Christ himself.

Hearken again, my beloved reader. Beware of mistakes as to the manner of coming to Christ. Dismiss from your mind for ever all idea of worthiness, merit, and fitness in yourself. Throw away notions of goodness, righteousness, and deserts. Think not that you can bring anything to recommend you, or to make you deserving of Christ's notice. You must come to him as a poor, guilty, undeserving sinner, or you might just as well not come at all. 'To him that worketh not, but believeth on him that justifieth the ungodly, his faith is counted for righteousness' (Romans 4:5). It is the peculiar mark of the faith that justifies and saves, that it brings to Christ nothing but an empty hand.

Hearken once more, my beloved reader. Let there be no mistake in your mind as to the special character of the man who has come to Christ, and is a true Christian. He is not an angel. He is not a half-angelic being, in whom is no weakness, or blemish, or infirmity. He is nothing of the kind. He is nothing more than a sinner who has found out his sinfulness, and has learned the blessed secret of living by faith in Christ. What was the glorious company of the apostles and prophets? What was the noble army of martyrs? What were Isaiah, Daniel, Peter, James, John, Paul, Polycarp, Chrysostom, Augustine, Luther, Ridley, Latimer, Bunyan, Baxter, Whitefield, Venn, Chalmers, Bickersteth, M'Cheyne?[3] What were they all, but sinners who knew and felt their sins, and trusted only in Christ? What were they but men who accepted the invitation I bring you this day, and came to Christ by faith? By this faith they lived. In this faith they died. In themselves and their doings they saw nothing worth mentioning. But in Christ they saw all that their souls required.

Reader, the invitation of Christ is now before you. If you never listened to it before, listen to it today. Broad, full, free, wide, simple, tender, kind— that invitation will leave you without excuse if you refuse to accept it. There are some Christmas invitations, perhaps, which it is wiser and better to decline. There is one which ought always to

[3] Polycarp of Smyrna, Chrysostom of Constantinople, Augustine of Hippo, Martin Luther, Nicholas Ridley, Hugh Latimer, John Bunyan, Richard Baxter, George Whitefield, Henry Venn, Thomas Chalmers, Edward Bickersteth, Robert Murray M'Cheyne.

be accepted. That one is before you today. Jesus Christ is saying, 'Come, come unto me.'

IV. I will now show you, in the last place, *what the Lord Jesus Christ promises to give*. He does not ask the labouring and heavy laden to come to him for nothing. He holds out gracious inducements. He allures them by sweet offers. 'Come unto me,' he says, 'and I will give you rest.'

Rest is a pleasant thing. Few are the men and women in this weary world who do not know the sweetness of it. The man who has been labouring hard with his hands all the week, working in iron, or brass, or stone, or wood, or clay—digging, lifting, hammering, cutting—he knows the comfort of going home on Saturday night, and having one day of rest. The man who has been toiling hard with his head all day—writing, copying, calculating, composing, scheming, planning—he knows the comfort of laying aside his papers and having a little rest. Yes! rest is a pleasant thing.

And rest is one of the principal offers which the gospel makes to man. Come to me, says the world, and I will give you riches and pleasure. Come with me, says the devil, and I will give you greatness, power, and wisdom. 'Come unto me,' says the Lord Jesus Christ, 'and I will give you rest.'

But what is the nature of that rest which the Lord Jesus promises to give? It is no mere repose of body. A man may have that and yet be miserable. You may place him in a palace, and surround him with every possible comfort. You may give him money in abundance, and everything that money can buy. You may free him from all care about tomorrow's bodily wants, and take away the need of labouring for a single hour. All this you may do to a man, and yet not give him true rest. Thousands know this only too well by bitter experience. Their hearts are starving in the midst of worldly plenty. Their inward man is sick and weary, while their outward man is clothed in purple and fine linen, and fares sumptuously every day! Yes! a man may have houses, and lands, and money, and horses, and carriages, and soft beds, and good fare, and attentive servants, and yet not have true rest.

The rest that Christ gives is an inward thing. It is rest of heart, rest of conscience, rest of mind, rest of affection, rest of will. It is rest, from a comfortable sense of sins being all forgiven and guilt all put away. It is rest, from a solid hope of good things to come, laid up beyond the reach of disease, and death, and the grave. It is rest, from the well-grounded feeling, that the great business of life is settled, its great end provided for, that in time all is well done, and in eternity heaven will be our home.

Rest such as this the Lord Jesus gives to those who come to him, by showing them his own finished work on the cross, by clothing them in his own perfect righteousness, and washing them in his own precious blood. When a man begins to see that the Son of God actually died for his sins, his soul begins to taste something of inward quiet and peace.

Rest such as this the Lord Jesus gives to those who come to him, by revealing himself as their ever-living high priest in heaven, and God reconciled to them through him. When a man begins to see that the Son of God actually lives to intercede for him, he will begin to feel something of inward quiet and peace.

Rest such as this the Lord Jesus gives to those who come to him, by implanting his Spirit in their hearts, witnessing with their spirits that they are God's children, and that old things are passed away, and all things are become new. When a man begins to feel an inward drawing towards God as a father, and a sense of being an adopted and forgiven child, his soul begins to feel something of quiet and peace.

Rest such as this the Lord Jesus gives to those who come to him, by dwelling in their hearts as king, by putting all things within in order, and giving to each faculty its place and work. When a man begins to find order in his heart in place of rebellion and confusion, his soul begins to understand something of quiet and peace. There is no true inward happiness until the true king is on his throne.

Rest such as this is the privilege of all believers in Christ. Some know more of it and some less. Some feel it only at distant intervals, and some feel it almost always. Few enjoy the sense of it without many a battle with unbelief, and many a conflict with fear. But all who truly come to Christ, know something of this rest. Ask them, with all their complaints and doubts, whether they would give up Christ and go back to the world. You will get only one answer. Weak as their sense of rest may be, they have got hold of *something* which does them good, and that *something* they cannot let go.

Rest such as this is within reach of all who are willing to seek it and receive it. The poor man is not so poor but he may have it. The ignorant man is not so ignorant but he may know it. The sick man is not so weak and helpless but he may get hold of it. Faith, simple faith, is the one thing needful in order to possess Christ's rest. Faith in Christ is the grand secret of happiness. Neither poverty, nor ignorance, nor tribulation, nor distress can prevent men and women feeling rest of soul, if they will only come to Christ and believe.

Rest such as this is the possession which makes men *independent*. Banks may break, and money make itself wings and flee away. War, pestilence, and famine may break in on a land, and the foundations of the earth be out of course. Health and vigour may depart, and the body be crushed down by loathsome disease. Death may cut down wife, and children, and friends, until he who once enjoyed them stands entirely alone. But the man who has come to Christ by faith, will still possess something which can never be taken from him. Like Paul and Silas, he will sing in prison.[4] Like Job, bereaved of children and property, he will bless the name of the Lord.[5] He is the truly independent man, who possesses that which nothing can take away.

Rest such as this is the possession which makes men truly *rich*. It lasts. It wears. It endures. It lightens the solitary home. It smooths down the dying pillow. It goes with men when they are placed in their coffins. It abides with them when they are

[4] Acts 16:25.
[5] Job 1:21.

laid in their graves. When friends can no longer help us, and money is no longer of use—when doctors can no longer relieve our pain, and nurses can no longer minister to our wants—when sense begins to fail, and eye and ear can no longer do their duty—then, even then, the 'rest' which Christ gives will be shed abroad in the heart of the believer. The words 'rich' and 'poor' will change their meaning entirely one day. He is the only rich man who has come to Christ by faith, and from Christ has received rest.

Reader, this is the rest which Christ offers to give to all who are labouring and heavy laden. This is the rest for which he invites them to come to him. This is the rest which I want you to enjoy, and to which I bring you a Christmas invitation this day. May God grant that the invitation may not be brought to you in vain!

(1) Reader, do you know anything of the 'rest' of which I have been speaking? If not, what have you got from your religion? You live in a Christian land. You profess and call yourself a Christian. You have probably attended a Christian place of worship many years. You would not like to be called an infidel or a heathen. Yet all this time what benefit have you received from your Christianity?

What solid advantage have you obtained from it?
For anything one can see, you might just as well
have been a Turk or a Jew.[6]

Take advice this day, and resolve to possess the
realities of Christianity as well as the name, and the
substance as well as the form. Do not be content
until you know something of the peace, and hope,
and joy, and consolation which Christians enjoyed
in former times. Ask yourself what is the reason
that you are a stranger to the feelings which men
and women experienced in the days of the apostles. Ask yourself why you do not 'joy in the Lord,'
and feel 'peace with God,' like the Romans and
Philippians, to whom St Paul wrote.[7] Religious
feelings, no doubt, are often deceptive. But surely
the religion which produces no feelings at all is
not the religion of the New Testament. The religion which gives a man no inward comfort, can
never be a religion from God. Reader, take heed
to yourself. Never be satisfied until you know
something of the 'rest that is in Christ.'

(2) Reader, do you desire rest of soul, and yet
know not where to turn for it? Remember this day,

[6] That is, religious monotheism like Islam or Judaism, but
without Christ.
[7] Philippians 4:4; Romans 5:1.

that there is only one place where it can be found. Governments cannot give it. Education will not impart it. Worldly amusements cannot supply it. Money will not purchase it. It can only be found in the hand of Jesus Christ, and to his hand you must turn, if you would find peace within.

There is no royal road to rest of soul. Let that never be forgotten. There is only one way to the Father, Jesus Christ—one door into heaven, Jesus Christ—and one path to heart-peace, Jesus Christ. By that way all labouring and heavy-laden ones must go, whatever be their rank or condition. Kings in their palaces and paupers in the work-house are all on a level in this matter. All alike must come to Christ, if they feel soul-weary and athirst. All must drink of the same fountain, if they would have their thirst relieved.

You may not believe what I am now writing. Time will shew who is right and who is wrong. Go on, if you will, imagining that true happiness is to be found in the good things of this world. Seek it, if you will, in revelling and banqueting, in dancing and merry-making, in races and theatres, in field-sports and cards. Seek it, if you will, in reading and scientific pursuits, in music and paint-ing, in politics and business. Seek it, but you will never overtake it, unless you change your plan.

Real heart-rest is never to be found except in heart-union with Jesus Christ.

The princess Elizabeth, daughter of Charles I, lies buried in Newport Church, in the Isle of Wight. A marble monument, erected by our gracious Queen Victoria, records in a touching way the manner of her death.[8] She languished in Carisbrooke Castle during the unhappy Commonwealth wars, a prisoner, alone, and separate from all the companions of her youth, until death set her free. She was found dead one day with her head leaning on her Bible, and the Bible open at the words, 'Come unto me, all ye that labour and are heavy laden, and I will give you rest.' The monument in Newport Church records this fact. It consists of a female figure reclining, her head on a marble book, with the text already quoted engraven on the book. Think, reader, what a sermon in stone that monument preaches! Think what a standing memorial it affords of the utter inability of rank and high birth to confer certain happiness! Think what a testimony it bears to the lesson before you this day—the mighty lesson

[8] Princess Elizabeth Stuart (1635–50) died of pneumonia, aged 14. Her marble monument, commissioned by Queen Victoria and designed by Baron Marochetti, was erected in St Thomas' Church, Newport, in 1856.

that there is no true rest for anyone excepting in Christ! Happy will it be for your soul if that lesson is never forgotten!

(3) Reader, do you desire to possess the rest that Christ alone can give, and yet feel afraid to seek it? I beseech you, as a friend to your soul, to cast this needless fear away. For what did Christ die on the cross, if not to save sinners? For what does he sit at the right hand of God, if not to receive and intercede for sinners? When Christ invites you so plainly, and promises so freely, why should you rob your own soul, and refuse to come to him?

Who among all the readers of this tract, desires to be saved by Christ, and yet is not saved at present? Come, I beseech you, come to Christ without delay. Though you have been a great sinner, come. Though you have long resisted warnings, counsels, sermons, come. Though you have sinned against light and knowledge, against a father's advice and a mother's tears, come. Though you have plunged into every excess of wickedness, and lived without a Sabbath and without prayer, yet come. The door is not shut. The fountain is not yet closed. Jesus Christ invites you. It is enough that you feel labouring and heavy laden, and desire to be saved. Come, come to Christ without delay.

Come to him by faith and pour out your heart before him in prayer. Tell him the whole story of your life, and ask him to receive you. Cry to him as the penitent thief did, when he saw him on the cross. Say to him, 'Lord, save me also. Lord, remember me.'[9]

Reader, if you have never come to this point yet, you must come to it at last, if you mean to be saved. You must apply to Christ as a sinner. You must have personal dealings with the great Physician, and apply to him for a cure. Why not do it at once? Why not this very Christmas accept the great invitation? Once more, I repeat my exhortation. Come, come to Christ without delay.

(4) Reader, have you found the rest which Christ gives? Have you tasted true peace by coming to him and casting your soul on him? Then go on to the end of your days as you have begun, looking to Jesus and living on him. Go on drawing daily full supplies of rest, peace, mercy, and grace from the great fountain of rest and peace. Remember that, if you live to the age of Methuselah, you will never be anything but a poor empty sinner, owing all you have and hope for to Christ alone.

[9] Luke 23:42.

Never be ashamed of living the life of faith in Christ. Men may ridicule and mock you, and even silence you in argument. But they can never take from you the feelings which faith in Christ gives. They can never prevent you feeling, 'I was weary till I found Christ, but now I have rest of conscience. I was blind, but now I see. I was dead, but I am alive again. I was lost, but I am found.'

Invite all around you to come to Christ. Use every lawful effort to bring father, mother, husband, wife, children, brothers, sisters, friends, relatives, companions, fellow-workmen, servants, to bring all and everyone to the knowledge of the Lord Jesus. Spare no pains. Speak to them about Christ: speak to Christ about them. Be instant in season, out of season. Say to them, as Moses did to Hobab, 'Come with us and we will do you good.'[10] The more you work for the souls of others, the more blessing will you get for your own soul.

Last, but not least, look forward with confidence to a better rest in a world to come. Yet a little time, and he that shall come, will come, and will not tarry. He will gather together all who have believed in him, and take his people to a home where the wicked shall cease from troubling, and

[10] Numbers 10:29.

the weary shall be at perfect rest. He shall give them a glorious body, in which they shall serve him without distraction, and praise him without weariness. He shall wipe away tears from all faces, and make all things new (Isaiah 25:8).

There is a good time coming for all who have come to Christ and committed their souls into his keeping. They shall remember all the way by which they have been led, and see the wisdom of every step in the way. They shall wonder that they ever doubted the kindness and love of their Shepherd. Above all, they shall wonder that they could be so long without him, and that when they heard of him they could hesitate about coming to him.

There is a pass in Scotland called Glen Croe, which supplies a beautiful illustration of what heaven will be to the man who comes to Christ. The road through Glen Croe carries the traveller up a long and steep ascent, with many a little winding and many a little turn in its course. But when the top of the pass is reached, a stone is seen by the wayside, with these simple words engraven on it, 'Rest, and be thankful.' Reader, those words describe the feelings with which everyone who comes to Christ will at length enter heaven. The summit of the narrow way will be won. We shall cease from our weary journeying, and sit down in the kingdom of God. We shall look back over all the way of life with thankfulness, and see the perfect wisdom of every little winding and turn in the steep ascent by which we were led. We shall forget the toils of the upward journey in the glorious rest. Here in this world our sense of rest in Christ at best is feeble and partial. But 'when that which is perfect is come, that which is in part shall be done away.'[11] Thanks be unto God, a day is coming when believers shall rest perfectly, and be thankful.

Reader, the Christmas invitation is now before you. Will you accept it?

[11] 1 Corinthians 13:10.

What Think Ye of Christ?
A Christmas Question

_____

'*What think ye of Christ?*'—Matthew 22:42

Reader,

Christmas is a season which almost all Christians observe in one way or another. Some keep it as a religious season. Some keep it as a holiday. But all over the world, wherever there are Christians, in one way or another Christmas is kept.

Perhaps there is no country in which Christmas is so much observed as it is in England. Christmas holidays, Christmas parties, Christmas family-gatherings, Christmas services in churches, Christmas hymns and carols, Christmas holly and mistletoe—who has not heard of these things? They are as familiar to English people as anything in their lives. They are among the first things we remember when we were children. Our grandfathers and grandmothers were used to them long before we were born. They have been going on in England for many hundred years. They seem likely to go on as long as the world stands.

But, reader, how many of those who keep Christmas ever consider *why Christmas is kept?* How many, in their Christmas plans and arrangements, give a thought to him, without whom there would have been no Christmas at all? How many ever remember that the Lord Jesus Christ is the cause of Christmas? How many ever reflect that the first intention of Christmas was to remind Christians of Christ's birth and coming into the world? Reader, how is it with you? What do you think of at Christmas?

Bear with me a few minutes, while I try to press upon you the question which heads this tract. I do not want to make your Christmas merriment less. I do not wish to spoil your Christmas cheer. I only wish to put things in their right places. I want Christ himself to be remembered at Christmas! Give me your attention while I unfold the question—'What think ye of Christ?'

I. Let us consider, firstly, *why all men ought to think of Christ.*

II. Let us examine, secondly, *the common thoughts of many about Christ.*

III. Let us count up, lastly, *the thoughts of true Christians about Christ.*

Reader, I dare say the demands upon your time this Christmas are many. Your holidays are short. You have friends to see. You have much to talk about. But still, in the midst of all your hurry and excitement, give a little time to your soul. There will be a Christmas some year, when your place will be empty. Before that time comes, suffer me, as a friend, to press home on your conscience the inquiry, 'What think ye of Christ?'

I. First, then, *let us consider why all men ought to think of Christ.*

This is a question which needs to be answered at the very outset of this tract. I know the minds of some people when they are asked about such things as I am handling today. I know that many are ready to say, 'Why should we think about Christ at all? We want meat, and drink, and money, and clothes, and amusements. We have no time to think about these high subjects. We do not understand them. Let parsons, and old women, and Sunday-school children mind such things if they like. We have no time in a world like this to be thinking of Christ.'

Such is the talk of thousands in this country. They never go either to church or chapel. They never read their Bibles. The world is their God. They think themselves very wise and clever. They despise those whom they call 'religious people.' But whether they like it or not, they will all have to die one day. They have all souls to be lost or saved in a world to come. They will all have to rise again from their graves, and to have a reckoning with God. And shall their scoffing and contempt stop our mouths, and make us ashamed? No, indeed! not for a moment! Listen to me and I will tell you why.

All men ought to think of Christ, because of *the office Christ fills between God and man*. He is the eternal Son of God, through whom alone the Father can be known, approached, and served. He is the appointed mediator between God and man, through whom alone we can be reconciled with God, pardoned, justified and saved. He is the divine person whom God the Father has sealed to be the giver of everything that man requires for his soul. To him are committed the keys of death and hell. In his favour is life. In him alone there is hope of salvation for mankind. Without him no child of Adam can be saved. 'Other foundation can no man lay than that is laid, which is Jesus Christ.' 'He that hath the Son hath life; and he that hath not the Son of God hath not life.'[1] And ought not man to think of Christ? Shall God the Father honour him, and shall not man? I tell every reader of this tract that there is no person, living or dead, of such immense importance to all men as Christ. There is no person that men ought to think about so much as Christ.

All men ought to think of Christ, because of *what Christ has done for all men.* He thought upon man, when man was lost, bankrupt, and helpless by the fall, and undertook to come into the world to save sinners. In the fulness of time he was born of the Virgin Mary, and lived for man thirty-three years in this evil world. At the end of that time he suffered for sin on the cross, as man's substitute. He bore man's sins in his own body, and shed his own life-blood to pay man's debt to God. He was made a curse for man, that man might be blessed. He died for man that man might live. He was counted a sinner for man that man might be counted righteous. And ought not man to think of Christ? I tell every reader of this tract that if Christ had not died for us, we might all of us, for anything we know, be lying at this moment in hell.

[1] 1 Corinthians 3:11; 1 John 5:12.

J. C. RYLE'S CHRISTMAS THOUGHTS

All men ought to think of Christ, because of *what Christ will yet do to all men.* He shall come again one day to this earth with power and glory, and raise the dead from their graves. All shall come forth at his bidding. Those who would not move when they heard the church-going bell, shall obey the voice of the archangel and the trump of God. He shall set up his judgment-seat, and summon all mankind to stand before it. To him every knee shall bow, and every tongue shall confess that he is Lord. Not one shall be able to escape that solemn assize. Not one but shall receive at the mouth of Christ an eternal sentence. Everyone shall receive according to what he has done in the body, whether it be good or bad. And ought not men to think of Christ? I tell every reader of this tract, that whatever he may choose to think now, a day is soon coming when his eternal condition will hinge entirely on his relations to Christ.

But why should I say more on this subject? The time would fail me if I were to set down all the reasons why all men ought to think of Christ. Christ is the grand subject of the Bible. The Scriptures testify of him. Christ is the great object to whom all the churches in Christendom profess to give honour. Even the worst and most corrupt branches of it will tell you that they are built on Christ. Christ is the end and substance of all sacraments and ordinances. Christ is the grand subject which every faithful minister exalts in the pulpit. Christ is the object that every true pastor sets before dying people on their deathbeds. Christ is the great source of light and peace and hope. There is not a spark of spiritual comfort that has ever illumined a sinner's heart, that has not come from Christ. Surely it never can be a small matter whether we have any thoughts about Christ.

Reader, I leave this part of my subject here. There are many things which swallow up men's thoughts while they live, which they will think little of when they are dying. Hundreds are wholly absorbed in political schemes, and seem to care for nothing but the advancement of their own party. Myriads are buried in business and money matters, and seem to neglect everything else but this world. Thousands are always wrangling about the forms and ceremonies of religion, and are ready to cry down everybody who does not use their shibboleths, and worship in their way. But an hour is fast coming when only one subject will be minded, and that subject will be Christ! We shall all find—and many perhaps too late—that it mattered little what we thought about other things, so long as we did not think about Christ.

Reader, I tell you this Christmas, that all men ought to think about Christ. There is no one in whom all the world has such a deep interest. There is no one to whom all the world owes so much. High and low, rich and poor, old and young, gentle and simple—all ought to think about Christ.

II. Let us examine, secondly, *the common thoughts of many about Christ.*

To set down the whole list of thoughts about Christ, would indeed be thankless labour. It must content us to range them under a few general heads. This will save us both time and trouble. There were many strange thoughts about Christ when he was on earth. There are many strange and wrong thoughts about Christ now, when he is in heaven.

The thoughts of some people about Christ are simply *blasphemous.* They are not ashamed to deny his divinity. They refuse to believe the miracles recorded of him. They pretend to find fault with not a few of his sayings and doings. They even question the perfect honesty and sincerity of some things that he did. They tell us that he ought to be ranked with great reformers and philosophers, like Socrates, Seneca, and Confucius, but no higher. Thoughts like these are purely ridiculous and absurd. They utterly fail to explain the enormous influence which Christ and Christianity have had for eighteen hundred years in this world. There is not the slightest comparison to be made between Christ and any other teacher of mankind that ever lived. The difference between him and others is a gulf that cannot be spanned, and a height that cannot be measured. It is the difference between gold and clay, between the sun and a candle. Nothing can account for Christ and Christianity, but the old belief that Christ is very God. Reader, are the thoughts I have just described your own? If they are, take care!

The thoughts of some people about Christ are *vague, dim, misty, and indistinct.* That there was such a person they do not for a moment deny. That he was the founder of Christianity, and the object of Christian worship, they are quite aware. That they hear of him every time they go to public worship, and ought to have some opinion or belief about him, they will fully admit. But they could not tell you what it is they believe. They could not accurately describe and define it. They have not thoroughly considered the subject. They have not made up their minds! Thoughts such as these are foolish, silly, and unreasonable. To be a dying sinner with an immortal soul, and to go on living without making up one's mind about the only person who can save us, the person who will at last judge us, is the conduct of a lunatic or an idiot, and not of a rational man. Reader, are the thoughts I have just described your own? If they are, take care!

The thoughts of some men about Christ are *mean and low*. They have no doubt a distinct opinion about his position in their system of Christianity. They consider that if they do their best, and live moral lives, and go to church pretty regularly, and use the ordinances of religion, Christ will deal mercifully with them at last, and make up any deficiencies. Thoughts such as these utterly fail to explain why Christ died on the cross. They take the crown off Christ's head, and degrade him into a kind of make-weight to man's soul. They overthrow the whole system of the gospel, and pull up all its leading doctrines by the roots. They exalt man to an absurdly high position; as if he could pay some part of the price of his soul! They rob man of all the comfort of the gospel; as if he must needs do something and perform some work to justify his own soul! They make Christ a sort of judge far more than a saviour, and place the cross and the atonement in a degraded and inferior position! Reader, are the thoughts I have just described your own? If they are, take care!

The thoughts of some men about Christ are *dishonouring and libellous.* They seem to think that we need a mediator between ourselves and our Saviour! They appear to suppose that Christ is so high, and awful, and exalted a person, that poor sinful man may not approach him! They say that we must employ an episcopally ordained minister as a kind of go-between, to stand between us and Jesus, and manage for our souls! They send us to saints, or angels, or the Virgin Mary, as if they were more kind and accessible than Christ! Thoughts such as these are a practical denial of Christ's priestly office. They overthrow the whole doctrine of his peculiar business, as man's intercessor. They hide and bury out of sight his especial love to sinners and his boundless willingness to receive them. Instead of a gracious Saviour, they make him out an austere and hard king. Reader, are the thoughts I have just described your own? If they are, take care!

The thoughts of some men about Christ are *wicked and unholy.* They seem to think that they may live as they please, because Christ died for sinners! They will indulge every kind of wickedness, and yet flatter themselves that they are not blameworthy for it, because Christ is a merciful Saviour! They will talk complacently of God's election, and the necessity of grace, and the impossibility of being justified by works, and the fulness of Christ, and then make these glorious doctrines an excuse for lying, cheating, drunkenness, fornication, and every kind of immorality. Thoughts such as these are as blasphemous and profane as downright infidelity. They actually make Christ the patron of sin. Reader, are these thoughts I have described your own? If they are, take care!

Reader, two general remarks apply to all these thoughts about Christ of which I have just been speaking. They all show a deplorable ignorance of Scripture. I defy anyone to read the Bible honestly, and find any warrant for them in that blessed book. Men cannot know their Bibles, when they hold such opinions. They all help to prove the corruption and darkness of human nature. Man is ready to believe anything about Christ except the simple truth. He loves to set up an idol of his own, and bow down to it, rather than accept the Saviour whom God puts before him.

I leave this part of my subject here. It is a sorrowful and painful one, but not without its use. It is necessary to study morbid anatomy, if we would understand health. The ground must be cleared of rubbish before we build.

III. Let us now count up, lastly, *the thoughts of true Christians about Christ.*

The thoughts I am going to describe are not the thoughts of many. I admit this most fully. It would be vain to deny it. The number of right thinkers about Christ in every age has been small. The true Christians among professing Christians have always been few. If it were not so, the Bible would have told an untruth. 'Strait is the gate,' says the Lord Jesus, 'and narrow is the way, that leadeth unto life, and few there be that find it. Wide is the gate, and broad is the way, that leadeth to destruction, and many there be which go in thereat.' 'Many walk,' says Paul, 'of whom I tell you, even weeping, that they are the enemies of the cross of Christ: whose end is destruction' (Matthew 7:13-14; Philippians 3:18-19).

True Christians have *high thoughts of Christ.* They see in him a wondrous person, far above all other beings in his nature—a person who is at one and the same time perfect God, mighty to save, and perfect man, able to feel. They see in him an all-powerful redeemer, who has paid their countless debts to God, and delivered their souls from guilt and hell. They see in him an almighty friend, who left heaven for them, lived for them, died for them, rose again for them, that he might save them for evermore. They see in him an almighty physician, who washed away their sins in his own blood, put his own Spirit in their hearts, delivered them from the power of sin, and gave them power to become God's children. Happy are they who have such thoughts! Reader, have you?

True Christians have *trustful thoughts of Christ*. They daily lean the weight of their souls upon him by faith, for pardon and peace. They daily commit the care of their souls to him, as a man commits a treasure to a safe keeper. They daily cling to him by faith, as a child in a crowd clings to its mother's hand. They look to him daily for mercy, grace, comfort, help, and strength, as Israel looked to the pillar of cloud and fire in the wilderness for guidance. Christ is the rock under their feet, and the staff in their hands, their ark and their city of refuge, their sun and their shield, their bread and their medicine, their health and their light, their fountain and their shelter, their portion and their home, their door and their ladder, their root and their head, their advocate and their physician, their captain and their elder brother, their life, their hope, and their all. Happy are they who have such thoughts! Reader, have you?

True Christians have *experimental thoughts of Christ*. The things that they think of him, they do not merely think with their heads. They have not learned them from schools, or picked them up from others. They think them because they have found them true by their own heart's experience. They have proved them, and tasted them, and tried them. They think what they have felt out for themselves. There is all the difference in the world between knowing that a man is a doctor or a lawyer, while we never have occasion to employ him, and knowing him as 'our own,' because we have gone to him for medicine or law. Just in the same way there is a wide difference between head knowledge and experimental thoughts of Christ. Happy are they who have such thoughts! Reader, have you?

True Christians have *loving and reverent thoughts of Christ*. They love to do the things that please him. They like in their poor weak way to show their affection to him by keeping his words. They love everything belonging to him, his day, his house, his ordinances, his people, his book. They never find his yoke heavy, or his burden painful to bear, or his commandments grievous. Love lightens all. They know something of the mind of Mr Standfast, in *Pilgrim's Progress*, when he said, as he stood in the river, 'I have loved to hear my Lord spoken of; and whenever I have seen the print of his shoe in the earth, then I have coveted to set my foot over it.'[2] Happy are they who have such thoughts! Reader, have you?

True Christians have *hopeful thoughts of Christ.* They expect yet to receive far more from him than they have ever received yet. They hope that they shall be kept to the end, and never perish. But this is not all. They look forward to Christ's second coming and expect that then they shall see far more than they have seen, and enjoy far more than they have yet enjoyed. They have the earnest of an inheritance now in the Spirit dwelling in their heart. But they hope for a far fuller possession when this world has passed away. They have hopeful thoughts of Christ's second advent, of their own resurrection from the grave, of their reunion with all the saints who have gone before them, of eternal blessedness in Christ's kingdom. Happy are they who have such thoughts! They sweeten life, and lift men over many cares. Reader, have you such thoughts?

Reader, thoughts such as these are the property of all true Christians. Some of them know more of them and some of them know less. But all know something about them. They do not

[2] John Bunyan, *The Pilgrim's Progress* (1678).

always feel them equally at all times. They do not always find such thoughts equally fresh and green in their minds. They have their winter as well as their summer, and their low tide as well as their high water. But all true Christians are, more or less, acquainted with these thoughts. In this matter churchmen and dissenters, rich and poor, all are agreed, if they are true Christians. In other things they may be unable to agree and see alike. But they all agree in their thoughts about Christ. One word they can all say, which is the same in every tongue. That word is 'Hallelujah,' praise to the Lord Christ! One answer they can all make, which in every tongue is equally the same. That word is, 'Amen,' so be it!

And now, reader, I shall wind up my Christmas tract, by simply bringing before your conscience the question which forms its title. I ask you this day, 'What think you of Christ?'

What others think about him, is not the question now. Their mistakes are no excuse for you. Their correct views will not save your soul. The point you have before you is simply this, 'What do you think yourself?'

Reader, this Christmas may possibly be your last. Who can tell but you may never live to see another December come round? Who can tell but your place may be empty, when the family party next Christmas is gathered together? Do not, I entreat you, put off my question or turn away from it. It can do you no harm to look at it and consider it. What do you think of Christ?

Begin, I beseech you, this day to have right thoughts of Christ, if you never had them before. Let the time past suffice you to have lived without real and heartfelt religion. Let this present Christmas be a starting point in your soul's history. Awake to see the value of your soul, and the immense importance of being saved. Break off sharp from sin and the world. Get down your Bible and begin to read it. Call upon the Lord Jesus Christ in prayer, and beseech him to save your soul. Rest not, rest not till you have trustful, loving, experimental, hopeful thoughts of Christ.

Reader, mark my words! If you will only take the advice I have now given you, you will never repent it. Your life in future will be happier. Your heart will be lighter. Your Christmas gatherings will be more truly joyful. Nothing makes Christmas meetings so happy, as to feel that we are all travelling on towards an eternal gathering in heaven.

Reader, I say for the last time, if you would have a happy Christmas, have right thoughts about Christ.

I remain,

Your affectionate friend,

J. C. Ryle

The Whole Family!

_____

'*The whole family in heaven and earth.*'
—Ephesians 3:15

Reader,

Look at the words which form the title of this tract, and ponder them well. They are words which ought to stir some feelings in our minds at any time, and especially at Christmas. There lives not the man or woman on earth who is not member of some 'family.' The poorest as well as the richest has his kith and kin, and can tell you something of his 'family.'

Family gatherings at Christmas, we all know, are very common. Thousands of firesides are crowded then, if at no other time of the year. The young man in town snatches a few days from business, and takes a run down to the old folks at home. The young woman in service gets a short holiday, and comes to visit her father and mother. Brothers and sisters meet for a few hours. Parents and children look one another in the face. How much there is to talk about! How many questions to be asked! How many interesting things to be told! Happy indeed is that fireside which sees gathered round it at Christmas 'the whole family'!

Family gatherings at Christmas are natural, and right, and good. I approve them with all my heart. It does me good to see them kept up. They are one of the very few pleasant things which have survived the fall of man. Next to the grace of God, I see no principle which unites people so much in this sinful world as family feeling. Community of blood is a most powerful tie. I have often observed that people will stand up for their relations, merely because they *are* their relations—and refuse to hear a word against them—even when they have no sympathy with their tastes and ways. Anything which helps to keep up family feeling ought to be commended. It is a wise thing, when it can be done, to gather together at Christmas 'the whole family.'

Family gatherings, nevertheless, are often sorrowful things. It would be strange indeed, in such a world as this, if they were not. Few are the family circles which do not show gaps and vacant places as years pass away. Changes and deaths make sad havoc as time goes on. Thoughts will rise up within us, as we grow older, about faces and voices no longer with us, which no Christmas merriment can entirely keep down. When the young members of the family have once begun to launch forth into the world, the old heads may long survive the scattering of the nest. But after a certain time, it seldom happens that you see together 'the whole family.'

And now, reader, let me take occasion from Christmas to tell you of a great family to which I want you to belong. It is a family despised by many, and not even known by some. But it is a family of far more importance than any family on earth. To belong to it entitles a man to far greater privileges than to be the son of a king. It is the family of which St Paul speaks to the Ephesians, when he tells them of the 'whole family in heaven and earth.' It is the family of God.

Reader, give me your attention while I try to describe this family, and recommend it to your notice. I do not wish to mar your Christmas merriment, or to lessen the joy of your Christmas gathering, wherever it may be. I only want to remind you of a better family, even a heavenly one, and of the amazing benefits which membership of that family conveys. I want you to be found one of that family, when its gathering shall come at last—a gathering without separation, or sorrow, or tears. Hear me while, as a minister of Christ, and friend to your soul, I talk for a few minutes about 'the whole family in heaven and earth':

I. First of all, *what is this family?*

II. Secondly, *what is its present position?*

III. Thirdly, *what are its future prospects?*

I wish to unfold these three things before you, and I invite your serious consideration of them. Our Christmas gatherings on earth must have an end one day. Our last earthly Christmas must come. Happy indeed is that Christmas which finds us prepared to meet God!

I. *What is that family* which the Bible calls 'the whole family in heaven and earth'? Of whom does it consist?

The family before us consists of all real Christians—of all who have the Spirit—of all true believers in Christ—of the saints of every age, and church, and nation, and tongue. It includes the blessed company of all faithful people. It is the same as the election of God—the household of faith—the mystical body of Christ—the bride—the living temple—the sheep that never perish—the church of the firstborn—the holy catholic church. All these expressions are only 'the family of God' under other names.

Membership of the family before us does not depend on any earthly connection. It comes not by natural birth, but by new birth. Ministers cannot impart it to their hearers. Parents cannot give it to their children. You may be born in the godliest family in the land, and enjoy the richest means of grace a church can supply, and yet never belong to the family of God. To belong to it you must be born again. None but the Holy Ghost can make a living member of his family. It is his special office and prerogative to bring into the true church such as shall be saved. They that are born again are born, 'not of blood, nor of the will of the flesh, nor of the will of man, but of God' (John 1:13).

Reader, do you ask the reason of this name which the Bible gives to the company of all true Christians? Would you like to know why they are called 'a family'? Listen, and I will tell you.

True Christians are called a 'family' because they have all *one Father*. They are all children of God by faith in Christ Jesus. They are all born of one Spirit. They are all sons and daughters of the Lord Almighty. They have received the Spirit of adoption, whereby they cry, Abba Father (Galatians 3:26; John 3:8; 2 Corinthians 6:18; Romans 8:15). They do not regard God with slavish fear, as an austere Being, only ready to punish them. They look up to him with tender confidence as a reconciled and loving parent, as one forgiving iniquity, transgression, and sin, to all who believe on Jesus, and full of pity even to the least and feeblest. The words, 'Our Father which art in heaven,' are no mere form in the mouth of true Christians. No wonder they are called God's 'family.'

True Christians are called 'a family,' because they all *rejoice in one name.* That name is the name of their great head and elder brother, even Jesus Christ the Lord. Just as a common family name is the uniting link to all the members of a Highland clan, so does the name of Jesus tie all believers together in one vast family. As members of outward visible churches they have various names and distinguishing appellations. As living members of Christ, they all, with one heart and mind, rejoice in one Saviour. Not a heart among them but feels drawn to Jesus as the only object of hope. Not a tongue among them but would tell you that 'Christ is all.' Sweet to them all is the thought of Christ's death for them on the cross. Sweet is the thought of Christ's intercession for them at the right hand of God. Sweet is the thought of Christ's coming again to unite them to himself in one glorified company for ever. In fact, you might as well take away the sun out of heaven, as take away the name of Christ from believers. To the world there may seem little in his name. To believers it is full of comfort, hope, joy, rest, and peace. No wonder they are called 'a family.'

True Christians, above all, are called 'a family' because there is so strong *a family likeness* among them. They are all led by one Spirit, and are marked by the same general features of life, heart, taste, and character. Just as there is a general bodily resemblance among the brothers and sisters of a family, so there is a general spiritual resemblance among all the sons and daughters of the Lord Almighty. They all hate sin and love God. They all rest their hope of salvation on Christ, and have no confidence in themselves. They all endeavour to come out and be separate from the ways of the world, and to set their affections on things above. They all turn naturally to the same Bible as the only food of their souls, and the only sure guide in their pilgrimage toward heaven. They find it a 'lamp to their feet, and a light to their path' (Psalm

119:105). They all go to the same throne of grace in prayer, and find it as needful to speak to God as to breathe. They all live by the same rule, the word of God, and strive to conform their daily life to its precepts. They have all the same inward experience. Repentance, faith, hope, charity, humility, inward conflict, are things with which they are all more or less acquainted. No wonder they are called 'a family.'

Reader, this family likeness among true believers is a thing that deserves special attention. To my own mind it is one of the strongest indirect evidences of the truth of Christianity. It is one of the greatest proofs of the reality of the work of the Holy Ghost. Some true Christians live in civilized countries, and some in the midst of heathen lands. Some are highly educated, and some are unable to read a letter. Some are rich and some are poor. Some are churchmen and some are dissenters. Some are old and some are young. And yet, notwithstanding all this, there is a marvellous oneness of heart and character among them. Their joys and their sorrows, their love and their hatred, their likes and their dislikes, their tastes and their distastes, their hopes and their fears, are all most curiously alike. Let others think what they please, I see in all this the finger of God. His handiwork is always one and the same. No wonder that true Christians are compared to 'a family.'

Take a converted Englishman and a converted Hindoo, and let them suddenly meet for the first time. I will engage, if they can understand one another's language they will soon find common ground between them, and feel at home. The one may have been brought up at school and college, and enjoyed every privilege of English civilization. The other may have been trained in the midst of gross heathenism, and accustomed to habits, ways, and manners as unlike the Englishman's as darkness compared to light. And yet now in half an hour they feel that they are friends! The Englishman finds that he has more in common with his Hindoo brother than he has with many an old college companion or school fellow! Who can account for this? How can it be explained? Nothing can account for it but the unity of the Spirit's teaching. It is 'one touch' of grace, not nature, 'that makes the whole world kin.'[1] God's people are in the highest sense 'a family.'

Reader, this is the family to which I wish to direct your attention this Christmas. This is the family to which I want you to belong. I ask you this

---

[1] William Shakespeare, *Troilus and Cressida* (1609).

day to consider it well, if you never considered it before. I have shown you the Father of the family, the God and Father of our Lord Jesus Christ. I have shown you the head and elder brother of the family, the Lord Jesus himself. I have shown you the features and characteristics of the family. Its members have all great marks of resemblance. Once more I say, consider it well.

Outside this family, remember, there is no salvation. None but those who belong to it, according to the Bible, are in the way that leads to heaven. The salvation of our souls does not depend on union with one church or separation from another. They are miserably deceived who think that it does, and will find it out to their cost one day, except they awake. No, reader, the life of our souls depends on something far more important. This is life eternal, to be a member of 'the whole family in heaven and earth.'

II. I will now pass on to the second thing which I promised to consider. *What is the present position* of 'the whole family in heaven and earth'?

The family to which I am directing your attention this day is divided into two great parts. Each part has its own residence or dwelling-place. Part of the family is in heaven, and part is on earth. For the present the two parts are entirely separated from one another. But they form one body in the sight of God, though resident in two places; and their union is sure to come one day.

Two places, be it remembered, and two only, contain the family of God. The Bible tells us of no third habitation. There is no such thing as purgatory, whatever some Christians may think fit to say. There is no house of training or probation for those who are not true Christians when they die. Oh no! There are but two parts of the family— the part that is seen and the part that is unseen, the part that is in 'heaven' and the part that is on 'earth.' The members of the family that are not in heaven are on earth, and those that are not on earth are in heaven. Two parts, and two only! Two places, and two only! Let this never be forgotten.

Some of God's family are safe *in heaven*. They are at rest in that place which the Lord Jesus expressly calls 'Paradise' (Luke 23:43). They have finished their course. They have fought their battle. They have done their appointed work. They have learned their lessons. They have carried their cross. They have passed through the waves of this troublesome world and reached the harbour. Little as we know about them we know that they are happy. They are no longer troubled by sin and temptation.

They have said goodbye for ever to poverty and anxiety, to pain and sickness, to sorrow and tears. They are with Christ himself, who loved them and gave himself for them, and in his company they must needs be happy (Philippians 1:23). They have nothing to fear in looking back to the past. They have nothing to dread in looking forward to things to come. Three things only are lacking to make their happiness complete. These three are the second advent of Christ in glory, the resurrection of their own bodies, and the gathering together of all believers. And of these three things they are sure.

Some of God's family are still *upon earth*. They are scattered to and fro in the midst of a wicked world, a few in one place and a few in another. All are more or less occupied in the same way, according to the measure of their grace. All are running a race, doing a work, warring a warfare, carrying a cross, striving against sin, resisting the devil, crucifying the flesh, struggling against the world, witnessing for Christ, mourning over their own hearts, hearing, reading, and praying, however feebly, for the life of their souls. Each is often disposed to think no cross so heavy as his own, no work so difficult, no heart so hard. But each and all hold on their way, a wonder to the ignorant world around them, and often a wonder to themselves.

But, reader, however divided God's family may be at present in dwelling-place and local habitation, it is still one family. Both parts of it are still one in character, one in possessions, and one in relation to God. The part in heaven has not so much superiority over the part on earth as at first sight may appear. The difference between the two is only one of degree.

Both parts of the family *love the same Saviour*, and delight in the same perfect will of God. But the part on earth loves with much imperfection and infirmity, and lives by faith not by sight. The part in heaven loves without weakness, or doubt, or distraction. It walks by sight and not by faith, and sees what it once believed.

Both parts of the family are *saints*. But the saints on earth are often poor weary pilgrims who find the 'flesh lusting against the spirit and the spirit lusting against the flesh, so that they cannot do the things they would' (Galatians 5:17). They live in the midst of an evil world, and are often sick of themselves and of the sin they see around them. The saints in heaven, on the contrary, are delivered from the world, the flesh, and the devil, and enjoy a glorious liberty. They are called 'the spirits of just men made perfect' (Hebrews 12:23).

Both parts of the family are *alike God's children.* But the children in heaven have learned all their lessons, have finished their appointed tasks, have begun an eternal holiday. The children on earth are still at school. They are daily learning wisdom, though slowly and with much trouble, and often needing to be reminded of their past lessons by chastisement and the rod. Their holidays are yet to come.

Both parts of the family are *alike God's soldiers.* But the soldiers on earth are yet militant. Their warfare is not accomplished. Their fight is not over. They need every day to put on the whole armour of God. The soldiers in heaven are all triumphant. No enemy can hurt them now. No fiery dart can reach them. Helmet and shield may both be laid aside. They may at last say to the sword of the Spirit, Rest and be still. They may at length sit down, and need not to watch and stand on their guard.

Last, but not least, both parts of the family are *alike safe and secure.* Wonderful as this may sound, it is true. Christ cares as much for his members on earth as his members in heaven. You might as well think to pluck the stars out of heaven, as to pluck one saint, however feeble, out of Christ's hand. Both parts of the family are alike secured by 'an everlasting covenant ordered in all things and sure' (2 Samuel 23:5). The members on earth, through the burden of the flesh and the dimness of their faith, may neither see, nor know, nor feel their own safety. But they are safe, though they may not see it. The whole family is 'kept by the power of God, through faith unto salvation' (1 Peter 1:5). The members yet on the road are as secure as the members who have got home. Not one shall be found missing at the last day. The words of the Christian poet shall be found strictly true:

> More happy, but not more secure,
> The glorified spirits in heaven.[2]

Reader, before I leave this part of my subject, I ask you to understand thoroughly the present position of God's family, and to form a just estimate of it. Learn not to measure its numbers or its privileges by what you see with your eyes. You see only a small body of believers in this present time. But you must not forget that a great company has got safe to heaven already, and that when all are assembled at the last day they will be 'a multitude which no man can number' (Revelation 7:9). You only see that part of the family which is struggling

[2] Augustus Montague Toplady, 'A Debtor to Mercy Alone' (1771).

on earth. You must never forget that the greater part of the family has got home and is resting in heaven. You see the militant part but not the triumphant. You see the part that is carrying the cross, but not the part which is safe in Paradise. The family of God is far more rich and glorious that you suppose. Believe me, it is no small thing to belong to the 'whole family in heaven and earth.'

III. I will now pass on to the last thing which I promised to consider. *What are the future prospects* of 'the whole family in heaven and earth'?

The future prospects of a family! What a vast amount of uncertainty these words open up when we look at any family now in the world! How little we can tell of the things coming on any of us! What a mercy that we do not know the sorrows, and trials, and separations through which our beloved children may have to pass, when we have left the world! It is a mercy that we do not know 'what a day may bring forth,' and a far greater mercy that we do not know what may happen in twenty years (Proverbs 27:1). Reader, foreknowledge of the future prospects of our belongings would spoil many a family gathering this Christmas, and fill the whole party with gloom.

Think how many a fine boy, who is now the delight of his parents, will by and by walk in the prodigal's footsteps, and never return home! Think how many a fair daughter, the joy of a mother's heart, will follow the bent of her self-will after a few years, and insist on some miserably mistaken marriage! Think how disease and pain will often lay low the loveliest of a family circle, and make her life a burden and weariness to herself, if not to others! Think of the endless breaches and divisions arising out of money matters! Alas! there is many a life-long quarrel about a few pounds, between those who once played together in the same nursery. Reader, think of these things! The 'future prospects' of many a family which meets together this Christmas are a solemn and serious subject. Hundreds, to say the least, are gathering together for the last time. When they part they will never meet again.

But, thank God, there is one great family whose prospects are very different. It is the family of which I am speaking in this tract, and commending to your attention. The future prospects of the family of God are not uncertain. They are good, and only good—happy, and only happy. Listen to me, and I will try to set them in order before you.

The members of God's family shall all be *brought safe home* one day. Here upon earth they may be scattered, tried, tossed with tempests, and bowed down with afflictions. But not one of them shall perish (John 10:28). The weakest lamb shall not be left to perish in the wilderness. The feeblest child shall not be missing when the muster-roll is brought out at the last day. In spite of the world, the flesh, and the devil, the whole family shall get home. 'If, when we were enemies, we were reconciled to God by the death of his Son, much more, being reconciled, we shall be saved by his life' (Romans 5:10).

The members of God's family *shall all have glorious bodies* one day. When the Lord Jesus Christ comes the second time the dead saints shall all be raised and the living shall all be changed. They shall no longer have a vile mortal body, full of weaknesses and infirmities. They shall have a body like that of their risen Lord, without the slightest liability to sickness and pain. They shall no longer be clogged and hindered by an aching frame when they want to serve God. They shall be able to serve him night and day without weariness, and to attend upon him without distraction. The former things will have passed away. That word will be fulfilled, 'I make all things new' (Revelation 21:5).

The members of God's family shall all be *gathered into one company* one day. It matters nothing where they have lived or where they have died. They may have been separated from one another both by time and space. One may have lived in tents, with Abraham, Isaac, and Jacob, and another travelled by railway in our own day. One may have laid his bones in an Australian desert, and another may have been buried in an English churchyard. It makes no difference. All shall be gathered together, from north and south, and east and west, and meet in one happy assembly to part no more. The earthly partings of God's family are only for a few days. Their meeting is for eternity. It matters little where we live. It is a time of scattering now, and not of gathering. It matters little where we die. All graves are equally near to Paradise. But it does matter much whether we belong to God's family. If we do we are sure to meet again at last.

The members of God's family shall all be *united in mind and judgment* one day. They are not so now about many little things. About the things needful to salvation there is a marvellous unity among them. About many speculative points in religion, about forms of worship and church government, they often sadly disagree. But there shall be no disagreement among them one day. Ephraim shall no longer vex Judah, nor Judah Ephraim. Church-men shall no more quarrel with dissenters, nor dissenters with churchmen. Partial knowledge and dim vision shall be at an end for ever. Divisions and separations, misunderstandings and misconstruc-tions, shall be buried and forgotten. As there shall only be one language, so there shall only be one opinion. At last, after six thousand years of strife and jangling, perfect unity and harmony shall be found. A family shall at length be shown to angels and men in which all are of one mind.

The members of God's family shall all be *perfected in holiness* one day. They are not literally perfect now. Though born again, and renewed after the image of Christ, they offend and fall short in many things (James 3:2). None know it better than they do themselves. It is their grief and sorrow that they do not love God more heartily and serve him more faithfully. But they shall be completely freed from all corruption one day. They shall rise again at Christ's second appearing without any of the infirmities which cleave to them in their lives. Not a single evil temper or corrupt inclination shall be found in them. They shall be presented by their head to the Father, without spot, or wrinkle, or any such thing—perfectly holy and without blemish—fair as the moon and clear as the sun (Ephesians 5:27; Canticles 6:10). Grace, even now, is a beautiful thing, when it lives, and shines, and flourishes in the midst of imperfection. But how much more beautiful will grace appear when it is seen pure, unmixed, unmingled, and alone. And it shall be seen so when Christ comes to be glorified in his saints in the last day.

Last, but not least, the members of God's family shall all be *eternally provided for* one day. When the affairs of this sinful world are finally wound up and settled, there shall be an everlasting portion for all the sons and daughters of the Lord Almighty. Not even the weakest of them shall be overlooked and forgotten. There shall be something for everyone, according to his measure. The smallest vessel of grace, as well as the greatest, shall be filled to the brim with glory. The precise nature of that glory and reward it would be folly to pretend to describe. It is a thing which eye has not seen, nor mind of man conceived. Enough for us to know that each member of God's family, when he awakes up after his Master's likeness, shall be satisfied (Psalm 17:15). Enough, above all, to know that their joy, and glory, and reward shall be for ever. What they receive in the day of the Lord they will never lose. The inheritance reserved for them, when they come of age, is 'incorruptible, undefiled, and fadeth not away' (1 Peter 1:4).

Reader, these prospects of God's family are great realities. They are not vague shadowy talk, of man's invention. They are real true things, and will be seen as such before long. They deserve your serious consideration. Examine them well.

Look round the families of earth with which you are acquainted, the richest, the greatest, the noblest, the happiest. Where will you find one among them all which can show prospects to compare with those of which you have just heard. The earthly riches, in many a case, will be gone in a hundred years hence. The noble blood, in many a case, will not prevent some disgraceful deed staining the family name. The happiness, in many a case, will be found hollow and seeming. Few, indeed, are the homes which have not a secret sorrow, or 'a skeleton in the closet.' Whether for present possessions or future prospects, there is no family so well off as 'the whole family in heaven and earth.' Whether you look at what they have now, or will have hereafter, there is no family like the family of God.

Reader, my task is done. My tract is drawing to a close. It only remains to close it with a few words of practical application. Give me your attention for the last time. May God bless what I am going to say to the good of your soul!

(1) I ask you a plain question. Take it with you to the family gathering which you are going to join at Christmas. Take it with you, and amidst all your Christmas happiness make time for thinking about it. It is a simple question, but a solemn one—*Do you yet belong to the family of God?*

To the family of God, remember! This is the point of my question. It is no answer to say that you are a Protestant, or a churchman, or a dissenter. I want to hear of something more and better than that. I want you to have some soul-satisfying and soul-saving religion—a religion that will give you peace while you live, and hope when you die. To have such peace and hope you must be something more than a Protestant, or a churchman, or a dissenter. You must belong to 'the family of God.' Thousands around you do not belong to it, I can well believe. But that is no reason why you should not.

If you do not yet belong to God's family, I invite you this day to join it without delay. Open your eyes to see the value of your soul, the sinfulness of sin, the holiness of God, the danger of your present condition, the absolute necessity of a mighty change. Open your eyes to see these things, and repent this very day. Open your eyes to see the great head of God's family, even Christ Jesus, waiting to save your soul. See how he has loved you, lived for you, died for you, risen again for you, and obtained complete redemption for you. See how he offers you free, full, immediate pardon, if you will believe in him. Open your eyes to see these things. Seek Christ at once. Come and believe on him, and commit your soul to his keeping this very day.

I know nothing of your family or past history. I know not where you go to spend your Christmas, or what company you are going to be in. But I am bold to say, that if you join the family of God this Christmas it will be the best and happiest Christmas in your life.

(2) Reader, if you really belong to the whole family in heaven and earth, count up your privileges, and *learn to be more thankful*. Think what a mercy it is to have something which the world can neither give nor take away—something which is independent of sickness or poverty—something which is your own for evermore. The old family fireside will soon be cold and tenantless. The old family gatherings will soon be past and gone for ever. The loving faces we now delight to gaze on

are rapidly leaving us. The cheerful voices which now welcome us will soon be silent in the grave. But, thank God, if we belong to Christ's family there is a better gathering yet to come. Let us often think of it and be thankful!

The family gathering of all God's people will make amends for all that their religion now costs them. A meeting where none are missing—a meeting where there are no gaps and empty places—a meeting where there are no tears—a meeting where there is no parting—such a meeting as this is worth a fight and a struggle. And such a meeting is yet to come to 'the whole family in heaven and earth.'

In the meantime let us strive to live worthy of the family to which we belong. Let us labour to do nothing that may cause our Father's house to be spoken against. Let us endeavour to make our Master's name beautiful by our temper, conduct, and conversation. Let us love as brethren, and abhor all quarrels. Let us behave as if the honour of the family depended on our behaviour.

So living, by the grace of God, we shall make our calling and election sure, both to ourselves and others. So living we may hope to have an abundant entrance, and to enter harbour in full sail, whenever we change earth for heaven. So living we shall recommend our Father's family to others, and perhaps, by God's blessing incline them to say, 'we will go with you.'

Reader, I commend these Christmas thoughts to your attention; and, wishing you a happy Christmas in the best and highest sense,

I remain,

Your affectionate friend,

J. C. Ryle

Without Christ!

'*That at that time ye were without Christ, being aliens from the commonwealth of Israel, and strangers from the covenants of promise, having no hope, and without God in the world.*'—Ephesians 2:12

Reader,

The return of Christmas has always something solemn about it. I do not envy that man who can see Christmas drawing near again without some serious thoughts.

One thought must surely come up in many minds at this season with peculiar power. That thought is about the many changes we have gone through since the first Christmas-day we can remember. Where are the happy homes where we used to assemble? Where are the happy faces which gathered round the old fireside? Where are the fathers, and mothers, and brothers, and sisters whom we used to meet at Christmas, if at no other time? In many cases there can only be one answer! The old homes are no more. The old family circles are broken up. The old loved relatives and friends have passed away. We are left alone. A few more years and we ourselves shall follow them. We too shall be gone.

But there are other thoughts which the return of Christmas should bring up in our minds, beside those which I have just mentioned. There is a home which is never broken up—a Father's house, in which there are many mansions—a house eternal in the heavens. There is a friend who sticketh closer than a brother—who never dies, never fails, never forsakes, never goes away. Reader, do you know anything yet of that unchanging friend and eternal home? Or does Christmas find you 'without any *home*,' except an earthly one, and without any friend that can help you beyond the grave? In one word—does Christmas find you 'without Christ'?

A Christmas without Christ! It cannot be a well-spent one. To talk of 'keeping Christmas' when he who was born of the Virgin Mary never enters into our thoughts, is surely nothing better than mockery. We are invited at this season to call to special remembrance the birth of the Lord Jesus Christ. But if our Christmas is nothing more than a merry-making and a holiday, and Jesus has no place in it, it can hardly be called 'well-spent.'

A Christmas without Christ! It cannot be a really happy one. There may be plenty of laughter, and merriment, and revelry. Music, and songs, and dancing, and feasting may make the hours pass pleasantly away. But if the Saviour, whose birth Christmas was intended to keep in mind, is not remembered and honoured, the joy is worth very little. There can be no true happiness 'without Christ.'

Reader, let me try to put before you a few thoughts which may help you to spend Christmas well. Let me suggest a few things which deserve consideration, because they affect your eternal interests. I do not want to lessen your Christmas happiness: on the contrary, I want to increase it. I only wish it to be real, true, solid, well-founded happiness. And I say boldly that there can be none 'without Christ.'

I. Let me first show you, *when it can be said of a man that he is 'without Christ.'*

II. Let me show you secondly, *what is the actual condition of a man 'without Christ.'*

Reader, do not throw this tract down, or turn away from it in contempt and disdain. Dare to look the subject in the face, and give it a few minutes of serious attention. Who can tell but it may prove a message from God to you? Who can tell but this very Christmas may be a turning-point in the history of your soul? A time must come in the life of every man who wishes to be saved, when he must turn to God, and set his face towards heaven. Reader, why not this very Christmas? Why not today?

I. *When can it be said of a man that he is 'without Christ'?*

The expression 'without Christ,' be it remembered, is not one of my own invention. The words were not first coined by me, but were written under the inspiration of the Holy Ghost. They were used by St Paul when he wrote his famous epistle to the Ephesian Christians. He was reminding them what their former condition was, before they heard the gospel and believed. Ignorant and dark no doubt they had been, buried in idolatry and heathenism, worshippers of the false goddess Diana. But all this he passes over completely. He seems to think that this would only partially describe their state. So he draws a picture, of which the very first feature is the expression before us: 'At that time ye were without Christ' (Ephesians 2:12). Now what does the expression mean?

A man is 'without Christ,' *when he has no head-knowledge of him.* Millions, no doubt, are in this condition. They neither know who Christ is—nor what he has done—nor what he taught—nor why he was crucified—nor where he is—nor what he is to mankind. In short, they are entirely ignorant of him. The heathen of course, who never yet heard the gospel come first under this description. But unhappily they do not stand alone. There are thousands of people living in England at this very day, who have no clearer ideas about Christ than the very heathen. Ask them what they know about Jesus Christ, and you will be astounded at the gross darkness which covers their minds. Visit them on their deathbeds, and you will find that they can tell you no more about Christ than about Mahomet. Thousands are in this state in country parishes, and thousands in towns. And about all such persons but one account can be given. They are 'without Christ.'

I am aware that some modern divines do not take the view which I have just stated. They tell us that all mankind have a part and interest in Christ, whether they know him or not. They say that all men and women, however ignorant while they live, shall be taken by Christ's mercy to heaven when they die! Such views, I firmly believe, cannot be reconciled with God's word. It is written, 'This is life eternal, that they might know thee, the only true God, and Jesus Christ whom thou hast sent' (John 17:3). It is one of the marks of the wicked, on whom God shall take vengeance at the last day, that they 'know not God' (2 Thessalonians 1:8). An unknown Christ is no Saviour. What shall be the state of the heathen after death—how the savage who never heard the gospel shall be judged—in what manner God will deal with the helplessly ignorant—all these are questions which we may safely let alone. We may rest assured that 'the Judge of all the earth will do right' (Genesis 18:25). But we must not fly in the face of Scripture. If Bible words mean anything, to be ignorant of Christ is to be 'without Christ.'

But this is not all. A man is 'without Christ' *when he has no heart-faith in him* as his Saviour. It is quite possible to know all about Christ, and yet not to put our trust in him. There are multitudes who know every article of the Belief, and can tell you glibly that Christ was 'born of the Virgin Mary, suffered under Pontius Pilate, was crucified, dead and buried.'[1] They learned it at school. They have it sticking fast in their memories. But they make no practical use of their knowledge. They put their trust in something which is not 'Christ.' They hope to go to heaven because they are moral and well-conducted—because they say their prayers, and go to church—because they have been baptized and go to the Lord's table. But as to a lively faith in God's mercy through Christ—a real, intelligent confidence in Christ's blood, and righteousness, and intercession, they are things of which they know nothing at all. And of all such persons I can see but one true account. They are 'without Christ.'

I am aware that many do not admit the truth of what I have just said. Some tell us that all baptized people are members of Christ by virtue of their baptism. Others tell us that where there is a head-knowledge, we have no right to question a person's interest in Christ. To these views I have only one plain answer. The Bible forbids us to say that any man is joined to Christ until he *believes*. Baptism is no proof that we are joined to Christ. Simon Magus was baptized, and yet was distinctly told that he had 'no part or lot in this

---

[1] The Apostles' Creed.

matter.'[2] Head-knowledge is no proof that we are joined to Christ. The devils know Christ well enough, but have no portion in him. God knows no doubt who are his from all eternity. But man knows nothing of any one's justification until he believes. The grand question is, 'Do we believe?' It is written, 'He that believeth not the Son shall not see life; but the wrath of God abideth on him.' 'He that believeth not shall be damned.' (John 3:36; Mark 16:16). If Bible words mean anything, to be without faith is to be 'without Christ.'

But I have yet one thing more to say. A man is 'without Christ' *when the Holy Spirit's work cannot be seen in his life.* Who can avoid seeing, if he uses his eyes, that myriads of professing Christians know nothing of inward conversion of heart. They will tell you that they believe the Christian religion. They go to their places of worship with tolerable regularity. They think it a proper thing to be married and buried with all the ceremonies of the church. They would be much offended if their Christianity were doubted. But where is the Holy Ghost to be seen in their lives? What are their hearts and affections set upon? Whose is the image and superscription that stands out in their

[2] Acts 8:21.

tastes, and habits, and ways? Alas! there can only be one reply. They know nothing experimentally of the renewing, sanctifying work of the Holy Ghost. They are yet dead to God. And of all such only one account can be given. They are 'without Christ.'

I am well aware that few will admit this. The vast majority will tell you that it is extreme, and wild, and extravagant to require so much in Christians, and to press on every one *conversion*. They will say that it is impossible to keep up the high standard which I have just referred to, without going out of the world; and that we may surely go to heaven without being such very great saints. To all this, I can only reply—What saith the Scripture? What saith the Lord? It is written, 'Except a man be born again, he cannot see the kingdom of God.' 'Except ye be converted, and become as little children, ye shall not enter into the kingdom of heaven.' 'He that saith he abideth in Christ, ought himself also so to walk, even as he walked.' 'If any man have not the Spirit of Christ, he is none of his' (John 3:3; Matthew 18:3; 1 John 2:6; Romans 8:9). The Scripture cannot be broken. If Bible words mean anything, to be without the Spirit is to be 'without Christ.'

Reader, I commend the three propositions I have just laid down to your serious and prayerful consideration. Mark well what they come to. Examine them carefully on every side. In order to have a saving interest in Christ, knowledge, faith, and the Holy Ghost are absolutely needful. He that is without them is 'without Christ'! Reader, are you?

How painfully ignorant are many! They know literally nothing about religion. Christ, and the Holy Ghost, and faith, and grace, and conversion, and sanctification, are mere 'words and names' to them. They could not explain what they mean, if it were to save their lives. And can such ignorance as this take anyone to heaven? Impossible! Without knowledge, 'without Christ'!

How painfully self-righteous are many! They can talk complacently about having 'done their duty,' and being 'kind to everybody,' and having always 'kept to their church,' and having 'never been so very bad' as some—and therefore, they seem to think, they must go to heaven! And as to deep sense of sin and simple faith in Christ's blood and sacrifice, it seems to have no place in their religion. Their talk is all of *doing*, and never of *believing*. And will such self-righteousness as this land anyone in heaven? Never! Without faith, 'without Christ'!

How painfully ungodly are many! They live in the habitual neglect of God's sabbath, God's Bible,

God's ordinances, and God's sacraments. They think nothing of doing things which God has flatly forbidden. They are constantly doing things that are directly contrary to God's commandments. And can such ungodliness end in salvation? Impossible! Without the Holy Ghost, 'without Christ'!

Reader, I know well that at first sight these statements seem hard, and sharp, and rough, and severe. But after all, are they not God's truth as revealed to us in Scripture? If truth, ought they not to be made known? If necessary to be known, ought they not to be plainly laid down? If I know anything of my own heart, I desire above all things to magnify the riches of God's love to sinners. I long to tell all mankind what a wealth of mercy and loving-kindness there is laid up in God's heart for all who will seek it. But I cannot find anywhere that ignorant, and unbelieving, and unconverted people have any part in Christ. If I am wrong, I shall be thankful to any one who will show me a more excellent way. But till I am shown it, I must stand fast on the positions I have already laid down. I dare not forsake them, lest I be found guilty of handling God's word deceitfully. I dare not be silent about them, lest the blood of souls be required at my hands. The man without knowledge, without faith, and without the Holy Ghost, is a man 'without Christ.'

II. Let me now turn to the second point which I promised to consider. *What is the actual condition of a man 'without Christ'?*

This is a branch of our Christmas subject that demands very special attention. Thankful indeed should I be if I could exhibit it in its true colours. I can easily imagine some reader saying to himself, 'Well! suppose I am without Christ, where is the mighty harm? I hope God will be merciful. I am no worse than many others. I trust all will be right at last.' Listen to me, and, by God's help, I will try to show that you are sadly deceived. 'Without Christ' all will not be right, but all desperately wrong.

For one thing, to be without Christ is to be *without God*. The Apostle St Paul told the Ephesians as much as this in plain words. He ends the famous sentence which begins, 'Ye were without Christ,' by saying, 'Ye were without God in the world.' And who that thinks can wonder? That man can have very low ideas of God who does not conceive him a most pure, and holy, and glorious, and spiritual being. That man must be very blind who does not see that human nature is corrupt, and sinful, and defiled. How then can such a worm as man draw near to God with comfort? How can he look up to him with confidence and not feel afraid? How can he speak to him, have dealings with him, look forward to dwelling with him, without dread and alarm? There must be a mediator between God and man, and there is but one that can fill the office. That one is Christ.

Who art thou that talkest of God's mercy and God's love separate from and independent of Christ? There is no such love and mercy recorded in Scripture. Know this day that God out of Christ is a consuming fire. Merciful he is, beyond all question, rich in mercy, plenteous in mercy. But his mercy is inseparably connected with the mediation of his beloved Son Jesus Christ. It must flow through him as the appointed channel, or it cannot flow at all. It is written, 'He that honoureth not the Son honoureth not the Father which hath sent him.' 'I am the way, the truth, and the life: no man cometh unto the Father but by me' (John 5:23; 14:6). 'Without Christ' we are without God.

For another thing, to be without Christ is to be *without peace*. Every man has a conscience within him, which must be satisfied before he can be truly happy. So long as this conscience is asleep or half dead, so long, no doubt, he gets along pretty well. But as soon as a man's conscience wakes up, and he begins to think of past sins, and present failings, and future judgment, at once he finds out that he needs something to give him inward rest. But what can do it? Repenting, and praying, and Bible-reading, and church-going, and sacrament-receiving, and self-mortification may be tried, and tried in vain. They never yet took off the burden from anyone's conscience. And yet peace must be had!

There is only one thing can give peace to the conscience, and that is the blood of Jesus Christ sprinkled on it. A clear understanding that Christ's death was an *actual payment* of our debt to God, and that the merit of that death is made over to man when he believes, is the grand secret of inward peace. It meets every craving of conscience. It answers every accusation. It calms every fear. It is written, 'These things I have spoken unto you, that in me ye might have peace.' 'He is our peace.' 'Being justified by faith, we have peace with God through our Lord Jesus Christ' (John 16:33; Ephesians 2:14; Romans 5:1). We have peace through the blood of his cross—peace like a deep mine—peace like an ever-flowing stream. But 'without Christ' we are without peace.

For another thing, to be without Christ is to be *without hope*. Hope of some sort or other almost every one thinks he possesses. Rarely indeed will you find a man who will boldly tell you that he has no hope at all about his soul. But how few there are that can give 'a reason of the hope that is in them'![3] How few can explain it, describe it, and show its foundations! How many a hope is nothing better than a vague, empty feeling, which the day of sickness and the hour of death will prove to be utterly useless—impotent alike to comfort or to save.

There is but one hope that has roots, life, strength and solidity, and that is the hope which is built on the great rock of Christ's work and office as man's Redeemer. 'Other foundation can no man lay than that is laid, which is Jesus Christ' (1 Corinthians 3:11). He that buildeth on this corner-stone 'shall not be confounded.' About this hope there is reality. It will bear looking at and handling. It will meet every enquiry. Search it through and through, and you will find no flaw whatever in it. All other hopes besides this are worthless. Like summer-dried fountains, they fail man just when his need is the sorest. They are like

[3] 1 Peter 3:15.

unsound ships, which look well so long as they lie quiet in harbour, but when the winds and the waves of the ocean begin to try them, their rotten condition is discovered, and they sink beneath the waters. There is to be no such thing as a good hope without Christ, and 'without Christ' is to have 'no hope' (Ephesians 2:12).

For another thing, to be without Christ is to be *without heaven*. In saying this I do not merely mean that there is no entrance into heaven, but that 'without Christ' there could be no happiness in being there. A man without a Saviour and Redeemer could never feel at home in heaven. He would feel that he had no lawful right or title to be there. Boldness and confidence and ease of heart would be impossible. Amidst pure and holy angels, under the eyes of a pure and holy God, he could not hold up his head. He would feel confounded and ashamed. It is the very essence of all true views of heaven that Christ is there.

Who art thou that dreamest of a heaven in which Christ has no place? Awake to know thy folly. Know that in every description of heaven which the Bible contains, the presence of Christ is one essential feature. 'In the midst of the throne,' says St John, 'stood a Lamb as it had been slain.' The very throne of heaven is called the 'throne of

God and of the Lamb.' 'The Lamb is the light of heaven, and the temple of it.' The saints who dwell in heaven are to be 'fed by the Lamb,' and 'led to living fountains of waters.' The meeting of the saints in heaven is called, 'the marriage supper of the Lamb' (Revelation 5:6; 22:3; 21:22-23; 7:17; 19:9). A heaven without Christ would not be the heaven of the Bible. To be 'without Christ' is to be without heaven.

Reader, I might easily add to these things, if time and space permitted. I might tell you that to be without Christ is to be without life, without strength, without safety, without foundation, without a friend in heaven, without righteousness. None so badly off as those that are without Christ!

What the ark was to Noah, what the passover lamb was to Israel in Egypt, what the manna, the smitten rock, the brazen serpent, the pillar of cloud and fire, the scape-goat, were to the tribes in the wilderness, all this the Lord Jesus is meant to be to man's soul. None so destitute as those that are without Christ!

What the root is to the branches, what the air is to our lungs, what food and water are to our bodies, what the sun is to creation, all this and much more Christ is intended to be to us. None so helpless, none so pitiable as those that are without Christ!

Reader, I grant that if there were no such things as sickness and death; if men and women never grew old, and lived on this earth for ever, the subject of this paper would be of no importance. But, you must know that sickness, death, and the grave, are sad realities.

If this life were all, if there were no judgment, no heaven, no hell, no eternity, it would be a mere waste of time to trouble yourself with such inquiries as this tract suggests. But, reader, you have got a conscience. You know well that there is a reckoning-day beyond the grave. There is a judgment yet to come.

Surely the subject of this tract is no light matter. It is not a small thing, and one that does not signify. It demands the attention of every sensible person. It lies at the very root of that all-important question, the salvation of our souls. To be 'without Christ' is to be most miserable.

(1) And now, reader, if you have read this tract through, I ask you *to examine yourself* and find out your own precise condition. Are you without Christ?

Do not allow Christmas to pass away without some serious thoughts and self-inquiry.

You cannot always go on as you do now. A day must come when eating, and drinking, and merry-making, will have an end. There will be a Christmas when your place will be empty, and you will be only spoken of as one dead and gone. And where will you be *then*, if you have lived and died without thought about your soul? Where will you be in another world, if your earthly Christmas has always been a Christmas without Christ? Oh! reader, it is better a thousand times to have a Christmas without money, and health, and friends, and company, and good cheer, than a Christmas without Christ.

(2) Reader, if you have lived without Christ hitherto, *I invite you* in all affection to change your course without delay. Seek the Lord Jesus while he can be found. Call upon him while he is near. He is sitting at God's right hand, able to save to the uttermost everyone who comes to him, however sinful and careless he may have been. He is sitting at God's right hand, willing to hear the prayer of everyone who feels that his past life has been all wrong, and wants to be set right. Seek Christ, reader, seek Christ without delay. Acquaint yourself with him. Do not be ashamed to apply to him. Only become one of Christ's friends this

Christmas, and you will say one day, it was the happiest Christmas that you ever had.

(3) Reader, if you have become one of Christ's friends already, *I exhort* you this Christmas to be a thankful man. Awake to a deeper sense of the infinite mercy of having an Almighty Saviour, a title to heaven, a home that is eternal, a friend that never dies! A few more years and all our Christmas gatherings will be over. What a comfort to think that we have in Christ something that we can never lose!

Awake to a deeper sense of the sorrowful state of those who are 'without Christ.' Christmas is a season when we are often reminded of the many who are without food, or clothing, or school, or church. Let us pity them, and help them, as far as we can. But let us never forget that there are people whose state is far more pitiable. Who are they? The people 'without Christ'!

Have we relatives 'without Christ'? Let us feel for them, pray for them, speak to the king about them, strive to recommend the gospel to them. Let us leave no stone unturned in our efforts to bring them to Christ.

Have we neighbours 'without Christ'? Let us labour in every way for their soul's salvation. The night cometh when none can work. Our last

Christmas will soon be here. Happy is he who lives under the abiding conviction that to be 'in Christ' is peace, safety, and happiness, and that to be 'without Christ' is to be on the brink of destruction.

Our Gathering Together!

'Now we beseech you, brethren, by the coming of our Lord Jesus Christ, and by our gathering together unto him.'—2 Thessalonians 2:1

THE text which heads this page contains a saying which deserves no common attention. It suits the month of December, the approach of Christmas, and the end of the year. That saying is, 'Our gathering together.'

Christmas is peculiarly a time when English people gather together. It is the season when family meetings have become almost a national institution. In town and in country, among rich and among poor, from the palace to the workhouse, Christmas cheer and Christmas parties are proverbial things. It is the one time in the twelve-month with many for seeing their friends at all. Sons snatch a few days from London business to run down and see their parents. Brothers get leave of absence from the desk to spend a week with their sisters. Friends accept long standing invitations, and contrive to pay a visit to their friends. Boys rush home from school, and glory in the warmth and comfort of the old house. Business for a little space comes to a standstill. The weary wheels of incessant labour seem almost to cease revolving for a few hours. In short, from the Isle of Wight to Berwick-on-Tweed there is a general spirit of 'gathering together.'

Happy is the land where such a state of things exists! Long may it last in England, and never may it end! Poor and shallow is that philosophy which sneers at Christmas gatherings. Cold and hard is that religion which pretends to frown at them, and denounces them as wicked. Family affection lies at the very roots of well ordered society. It is one of the few good things which have survived the fall, and prevent men and women from being mere devils. It is the secret oil on the wheels of our social system which keeps the whole machine going, and without which neither steam nor fire would avail. Anything which helps to keep up family affection and brotherly love, is a positive good to a country. May the Christmas day never arrive in England when there are no family meetings and no gatherings together!

But earthly gatherings after all have something about them that is sad and sorrowful. The happiest parties sometimes contain uncongenial members. The merriest meetings are only for a very short time. Moreover, as years roll on, the hand of death makes painful gaps in the family circle. Even in the midst of Christmas merriment we cannot help remembering those who have passed away. The longer we live, the more we feel to stand alone. The old faces will rise before the eyes of our minds, and the old voices will sound in our ears, even in the midst of holiday mirth and laughter. People do not talk much of such things; but there are few that do not feel them. We need not intrude our inmost thoughts on others, and especially when all around us are bright and happy. But there are not many, I suspect, who reach middle age, who would not admit, if they spoke the truth, that there are sorrowful things inseparably mixed up with a Christmas party. In short, there is no unmixed pleasure about any earthly gathering.

But is there no better gathering yet to come? Is there no bright prospect in our horizon of an assembly which shall far outshine the assemblies of Christmas and New Year—an assembly in which there shall be joy without sorrow and mirth without tears? I thank God that I can give a plain answer to these questions; and to give it is the simple object of this tract. Reader, lend me your attention for a few minutes, and I will soon show you what I mean.

I. There is a gathering together of true Christians which is yet to come. *What is it, and when shall it be?*

The gathering I speak of shall take place at the end of the world, in the day when Christ returns to earth the second time. As surely as he came the first time, so surely shall he come the second time. In the clouds of heaven he went away, and in the clouds of heaven he shall return. Visibly, in the body, he went away, and visibly, in the body, he will return. And the very first thing that Christ will do will be to gather together his people. 'He shall send his angels with a great sound of a trumpet, and they shall gather together his elect from the four winds, from one end of heaven to the other' (Matthew 24:31).

The *manner* of this 'gathering together' is plainly revealed in Scripture. The dead saints shall all be raised, and the living saints shall all be changed. It is written, 'The sea shall give up the dead which are in it, and death and hell shall give up the dead that are in them.' 'The dead in Christ shall rise first.

Those which are alive and remain shall be caught up together with them in the clouds, to meet the Lord in the air.' 'We shall not all sleep, but we shall all be changed, in a moment, in the twinkling of an eye, at the last trump: for the trumpet shall sound, and the dead shall be raised incorruptible, and we shall be changed.' (Revelation 20:13; 1 Thessalonians 4:16-17; 1 Corinthians 15:51-52.) And then, when every member of Christ is found, and not one left behind, when soul and body, those old companions, are once more reunited, then shall be the grand 'gathering together.'

The *object* of this 'gathering together' is as clearly revealed in Scripture as its manner. It is partly for the final reward of Christ's people, that their complete justification from all guilt may be declared to all creation, that they may receive the crown of glory which fadeth not away, and the kingdom prepared before the foundation of the world, that they may be admitted publicly into the joy of their Lord. It is partly for the safety of Christ's people, that, like Noah in the ark and Lot in Zoar, they may be hid and covered before the storm of God's judgment comes down on the wicked, that when the last plagues are falling on the enemies of the Lord, they may be untouched, as Rahab's family in the fall of Jericho, and unscathed as the three children in the midst of the fire. The saints have no cause to fear the day of gathering, however fearful the signs that may accompany it. Before the final crash of all things begins, they shall be hidden in the secret place of the Most High. The grand gathering is for their safety and their reward. 'Fear not ye,' shall the angel-reapers say, 'for ye seek Jesus, which was crucified.'[1] 'Come, my people,' shall their Master say, 'enter into thy chambers, and shut thy door about thee: hide thyself as it were for a little moment, until the indignation be overpast' (Isaiah 26:20).

This gathering will be a *great* one. All children of God who have ever lived, from Abel the first saint down to the last born in the day that our Lord comes—all of every age, and nation, and church, and people, and tongue—all shall be assembled together. Not one shall be overlooked or forgotten. The weakest and feeblest shall not be left behind. Now, when scattered, true Christians seem a little flock; then, when gathered, they shall be found a multitude which no man can number.

This gathering will be a *wonderful* one. The saints from distant lands, who never saw each other in the flesh, and could not understand each

---

[1] Matthew 28:5.

other's speech if they met, shall all be brought together in one harmonious company. The dwellers in Australia shall find they are as near heaven, and as soon there as the dwellers in England. The believers who died five thousand years ago, and whose bones are mere dust, shall find their bodies raised and renewed as quickly as those who are alive when the trumpet sounds. Above all, miracles of grace will be revealed. We shall see some in heaven who we never expected would have been saved at all. The confusion of tongues shall at length be reversed, and done away. The assembled multitude will cry with one heart and in one language, 'What hath God wrought!'[2]

This gathering shall be a *humbling* one. It shall make an end of bigotry and narrow-mindedness for ever. The Christians of one denomination shall find themselves side by side with those of another denomination. If they would not tolerate them on earth, they will be obliged to tolerate them in heaven. Churchmen and dissenters who will neither pray together nor worship together now, will discover to their shame, that they must praise together hereafter to all eternity. The very people who will not receive us at their ordinances now,

[2] Numbers 23:23.

and keep us back from their table, will be obliged to acknowledge us before our Master's face, and to let us sit down by their side. Never will the world have seen such a complete overthrow of sectarianism, party-spirit, unbrotherliness, religious jealousy, and religious pride. At last we shall all be completely 'clothed with humility.'[3]

Reader, this mighty, wonderful 'gathering together,' is the gathering which ought to be often in men's thoughts. It deserves consideration; it demands attention. Gatherings of other kinds are incessantly occupying our minds: political gatherings, scientific gatherings, gatherings for pleasure, gatherings for gain. But the hour comes, and will soon be here, when gatherings of this kind will be completely forgotten. One thought alone will swallow up men's minds. That thought will be, 'Shall I be gathered with Christ's people into a place of safety and honour, or be left behind to everlasting woe?' Reader, take care that you are not left behind.

II. *Why is this 'gathering together' of true Christians a thing to be desired?* Let us try to get an answer to that question.

[3] 1 Peter 5:5.

St Paul evidently thought that the gathering at the last day was a cheering object which Christians ought to keep before their eyes. He classes it with that second coming of our Lord, which he says elsewhere believers love and long for. He exalts it in the distant horizon as one of those 'good things to come,' which should animate the faith of every pilgrim in the narrow way. Not only, he seems to say, will each servant of God have rest, and a kingdom, and a crown: he will have besides a happy gathering together. Now where is the peculiar blessedness of this gathering? Why is it a thing that we ought to look forward to with joy, and expect with pleasure? Let us see.

For one thing, the gathering together of all true Christians will be a *state of things totally unlike their present condition.* To be scattered and not gathered, seems the rule of man's existence now. Of all the millions who are annually born into the world, how few continue together till they die. Children who draw their first breath under the same roof, and play by the same fireside, are sure to be separated as they grow up, and to draw their last breath far distant from one another. The same law applies to the people of God. They are spread abroad like salt, one in one place and one in another, and never allowed to continue long side by side. It is doubtless good for the world that it is so. A town would be a very dark place at night if all the lighted candles were crowded together into one room. But good as it is for the world, it is no small trial to believers. Many a day they feel desolate and alone. Many a day they long for a little more communion with their brethren, and a little more companionship with those who love the Lord. Well! they may look forward with hope and comfort. The hour is coming when they shall have no lack of companions. Let them lift up their heads and rejoice. There will be a gathering together by and by.

For another thing, the gathering together of all true Christians will be *an assembly entirely of one mind*. There are no such assemblies now. Mixture, hypocrisy, and false profession, creep in everywhere. Wherever there is wheat there are sure to be tares. Wherever there are good fish there are sure to be bad. Wherever there are wise virgins there are sure to be foolish. There is no such thing as a perfect Church now. There is a Judas Iscariot at every communion table, and a Demas in every apostolic company; and wherever the sons of God come together, Satan is sure to appear among them. But all this shall come to an end one day. Our Lord shall at length present to the Father a perfect church, having neither spot nor wrinkle, nor any such thing.[4] How glorious such a church will be! To meet with half-a-dozen believers together now is a rare event in a Christian's year, and one that cheers him like a sunshiny day in winter. It makes him feel his heart burn within him, as the disciples felt on the way to Emmaus. But how much more joyful will it be to meet a multitude that no man can number! To find too, that all we meet are at last of one opinion and one judgment, and see eye to eye—to discover that all our miserable controversies are buried for ever, and that Calvinists no longer hate Arminians, nor Arminians Calvinists, churchmen no longer quarrel with dissenters, nor dissenters with churchmen—to join a company of Christians in which there is neither jarring, squabbling, nor discord—every man's graces fully developed, and every man's besetting sins dropped off like beech-leaves in spring—all this will be happiness indeed. No wonder that St Paul bids us look forward.

For another thing, the gathering together of true Christians will be *a meeting at which none shall be absent*. The weakest lamb shall not be left behind in the wilderness. The youngest babe that ever

---

[4] Ephesians 5:27.

drew breath shall not be overlooked or forgotten. We shall once more see our beloved friends and relatives who fell asleep in Christ, and left us in sorrow and tears—better, brighter, more beautiful, more pleasant than ever we found them on earth. We shall hold communion with all the saints of God who have fought the good fight before us, from the beginning of the world to the end. Patriarchs and prophets, apostles and fathers, martyrs and missionaries, reformers and puritans, all the host of God's elect shall be there. If to read their words and works has been pleasant, how much better shall it be to see them! If to hear of them, and be stirred by their example, has been useful, how much more delightful to talk with them, and ask them questions! To sit down with Abraham, Isaac, and Jacob, and hear how they kept the faith without any Bible—to converse with Moses, and Samuel, and David, and Isaiah, and Daniel, and hear how they could believe in Christ yet to come—to converse with Peter, and Paul, and Lazarus, and Mary, and Martha, and listen to their wondrous tale of what their Master did for them—all this will be sweet indeed! No wonder that St Paul bids us look forward.

In the last place, the gathering of all true Christians shall be *a meeting without a parting*. There are no such meetings now. We seem to live in an endless hurry, and can hardly sit down and take breath before we are off again. 'Goodbye' treads on the heels of 'How do you do?' The cares of this world, the necessary duties of life, the demands of our families, the work of our various stations and callings—all these things appear to eat up our days, and to make it impossible to have long quiet times of communion with God's people. But, blessed be God, it shall not always be so. The hour cometh and shall soon be here, when 'goodbye' and 'farewell' shall be words that are laid aside and buried for ever. When we meet in a world where the former things have passed, where there is no more sin and no more sorrow—no more poverty and no more money—no more work of body or work of brains—no more need of anxiety for families—no more sickness, no more pain, no more old age, no more death, no more change—when we meet in that endless state of being, calm and restful, and unhurried—who can tell what the blessedness of the change will be? I cannot wonder that St Paul bids us look up and look forward.

Reader, I lay these things before you, and ask your serious attention to them. If I know anything of a Christian's experience, I am sure they contain food for reflection. This, at least, I say confidently:

the man who sees nothing much in the coming
of Christ and the public gathering of Christ's
people—nothing happy, nothing joyful, nothing
pleasant, nothing desirable—such a man may well
doubt whether he himself is a true Christian and
has got any grace at all.

(1) Reader, *I ask you a Christmas question.* Do
not turn away from it and refuse to look it in
the face. Shall you be gathered by the angels into
God's home when the Lord returns, or shall you
be left behind?

One thing, at any rate, is very certain. There
will only be two parties of mankind at the last
great day: those who are on the right hand of
Christ, and those who are on the left—those
who are counted righteous, and those who are
wicked—those who are safe in the ark, and those
who are outside—those who are gathered like
wheat into God's barn, and those who are left
behind like tares to be burned. Now, what will
your portion be?

Perhaps you do not know yet. You cannot say.
You are not sure. You hope the best. You trust it
will be all right at last: but you won't undertake
to give an opinion. Well! I only hope you will
never rest till you do know. The Bible will tell

you plainly who are they that will be gathered. Your own heart, if you deal honestly, will tell you whether you are one of the number. Rest not, rest not, till you know!

How men can stand the partings and separations of this life if they have no hope of anything better—how they can bear to say goodbye to sons and daughters, and launch them on the troublesome waves of this world, if they have no expectation of a safe gathering in Christ at last—how they can part with beloved members of their families, and let them journey forth to the other side of the globe, not knowing if they shall ever meet happily in this life or a life to come—how all this can be completely baffles my understanding! I can only suppose that the many never think, never consider, never look forward. Once let a man begin to think, and he will never be satisfied till he has found Christ and is safe.

(2) Reader, *I offer you a plain means of testing your own soul's condition this Christmas*, if you want to know your own chance of being gathered into God's home. Ask yourself what kind of gatherings you like best here upon earth? Ask yourself whether you really love the assembling together of God's people?

How could that man enjoy the meeting of true Christians in heaven who takes no pleasure in meeting true Christians on earth? How can that heart which is wholly set on balls, and races, and feasts, and amusements, and worldly assemblies, and thinks earthly worship a weariness—how can such a heart be in tune for the company of saints and saints alone? The thing is impossible. It cannot be.

Never, never let it be forgotten, that our tastes on earth are a sure evidence of the state of our hearts; and the state of our hearts here is a sure indication of our position hereafter. Heaven is a prepared place for a prepared people. He that hopes to be gathered with saints in heaven while he only loves the gathering of sinners on earth is deceiving himself. If he lives and dies in that state of mind, he will find at last that he had better never have been born.

(3) If you are a true Christian, *I exhort you this Christmas to be often looking forward.* Your good things are yet to come. Your redemption draweth nigh. The night is far spent. The day is at hand. Yet a little time, and he whom you love and believe on will come, and will not tarry. When he comes, he will bring his dead saints with him and change his

living ones. Look forward! There is a 'gathering together' yet to come.

Does Christmas bring with it sorrowful feelings and painful associations? Do tears rise unbidden in your eyes, when you mark the empty places round the fireside? Do grave thoughts come sweeping over your mind, even in the midst of your children's mirth, when you recollect the dear old faces and much loved voices of some that sleep in the churchyard? Well, look up and look forward! The time is short. The world is growing old. The coming of the Lord draweth nigh. There is yet to be a meeting without parting, and a gathering without separation. Those believers whom you laid in the grave with many tears are in good keeping. You will yet see them again with joy. Look up! I say once more. Lay hold by faith on the 'coming of our Lord Jesus Christ, and our gathering together unto him.' Believe it, think of it, rest on it. It is all true.

Do you feel lonely and desolate as every December comes round? Do you find few to pray with, few to praise with, few to open your heart to, few to exchange experience with? Do you learn increasingly, that heaven is becoming every year more full and earth more empty? Well, it is an old story. You are only drinking a cup which myriads have drunk before. Look up and look forward. The lonely time will soon be past and over. You will have company enough by and by. When you awake up after your Lord's likeness you shall be satisfied.[5] Yet a little while, and you shall see a congregation that shall never break up, and a sabbath that shall never end. 'The coming of our Lord Jesus Christ, and our gathering together unto him,' shall make amends for all.

———

[5] Psalm 17:15.

A Note on Sources

The Christmas tracts reproduced in this edition are Ryle's earliest surviving versions, as follows:

• *'Come!' A Christmas Invitation. Being Thoughts on Matt xi. 28* (Ipswich: William Hunt, 1859), second edition, tenth thousand. Copy at Widener Library, Harvard University.

• *What Think Ye of Christ? A Christmas Question for 1863* (London: William Hunt and Company, 1863), first edition. Copy at Cambridge University Library.

• *The Whole Family! A Tract for Christmas. Being Thoughts on Ephes iii. 15* (London: William Hunt and Company, 1864), first edition. Copy at Beinecke Library, Yale University.

• *Without Christ! A Tract for Christmas. Being Thoughts on Ephes ii. 12* (London: William Hunt

and Company, 1865), second edition, tenth thousand. Copy at Cambridge University Library.

• *Our Gathering Together! A Tract for Christmas.
Being Thoughts on II Thes ii. 1* (London: William
Hunt and Company, 1868), first edition. Copy in
possession of Andrew Atherstone.

Ryle wrote hundreds of tracts, which he often
revised and republished in different formats and
compilations. Some of his Christmas tracts were
reproduced in later volumes, though with the orig-
inal Christmas context diluted or entirely deleted.
Come! reappeared as 'Christ's Invitation' in *Old
Paths* (1877). *The Whole Family!* and *Our Gathering
Together!* reappeared as 'The Family of God' and
'The Great Gathering' in *Practical Religion* (1878).
Without Christ! reappeared, in abridged form, as a
chapter in *Holiness* (1879).

BANNER
of **TRUTH**

J. C. Ryle's compilation volumes are available in new editions from the Banner of Truth Trust:

Charges and Addresses

Christian Leaders of the Eighteenth Century

Expository Thoughts on the Gospels, 7 vols

Holiness

Knots Untied

Light from Old Times

Old Paths

Practical Religion

The Upper Room

Also available from the Trust:

Bishop J. C. Ryle's Autobiography: The Early Years, edited by Andrew Atherstone

J. C. Ryle: Prepared to Stand Alone, Iain H. Murray